Whose
Community?
Which
Interpretation?

THE CHURCH
AND POSTMODERN
CULTURE

James K. A. Smith, series editor
www.churchandpomo.org

The Church and Postmodern
Culture series features high-profile
theorists in continental philosophy
and contemporary theology
writing for a broad, nonspecialist
audience interested in the impact of
postmodern theory on the faith and
practice of the church.

Also available in the series

James K. A. Smith, *Who's Afraid of Postmodernism? Taking Derrida, Lyotard, and Foucault to Church*

John D. Caputo, *What Would Jesus Deconstruct? The Good News of Postmodernism for the Church*

Carl Rashke, *GloboChrist: The Great Commission Takes a Postmodern Turn*

Graham Ward, *The Politics of Discipleship: Becoming Post-material Citizens*

Whose Community? Which Interpretation?

Philosophical Hermeneutics for the Church

Merold Westphal

B

Baker Academic

a division of Baker Publishing Group
Grand Rapids, Michigan

© 2009 by Merold Westphal

Published by Baker Academic
a division of Baker Publishing Group
P.O. Box 6287, Grand Rapids, MI 49516-6287
www.bakeracademic.com

Printed in the United States of America

Library of Congress Cataloging-in-Publication Data
Westphal, Merold.
    Whose community? which interpretation? : philosophical hermeneutics for the church / Merold Westphal.
        p.   cm. — (The church and postmodern culture)
    Includes bibliographical references and index.
    ISBN 978-0-8010-3147-2 (pbk.)
    1. Bible—Hermeneutics. 2. Hermeneutics—Religious aspects—Christianity. 3. Gadamer, Hans-Georg, 1900–2002. I. Title.
BS476.W475 2009
220.601—dc22   2009006705

Contents

Series Preface

Current discussions in the church—from emergent "postmodern" congregations to mainline "missional" congregations—are increasingly grappling with philosophical and theoretical questions related to postmodernity. In fact, it could be argued that developments in postmodern theory (especially questions of "post-foundationalist" epistemologies) have contributed to the breakdown of former barriers between evangelical, mainline, and Catholic faith communities. Postliberalism—a related "effect" of postmodernism—has engendered a new, confessional ecumenism wherein we find nondenominational evangelical congregations, mainline Protestant churches, and Catholic parishes all wrestling with the challenges of postmodernism and drawing on the culture of postmodernity as an opportunity for rethinking the shape of our churches.

This context presents an exciting opportunity for contemporary philosophy and critical theory to "hit the ground," so to speak, by allowing high-level work in postmodern theory to serve the church's practice—including all the kinds of congregations and communions noted above. The goal of this series is to bring together high-profile theorists in continental philosophy and contemporary theology to write for a broad, nonspecialist audience interested in the impact of postmodern theory on the faith and practice of the church. Each book in the series will, from different angles and with different questions, undertake to answer questions such as What does postmodern theory have to say about the shape of the church? How should concrete, in-the-pew and on-the-ground religious practices be impacted by postmodernism? What should the church look like in postmodernity? What has Paris to do with Jerusalem?

The series is ecumenical not only with respect to its ecclesial destinations but also with respect to the facets of continental philosophy and theory that are represented. A wide variety of theoretical commitments will be included, ranging from deconstruction to Radical Orthodoxy, including voices from Badiou to Žižek and the usual suspects in between (Nietzsche, Heidegger, Levinas, Derrida, Foucault, Irigaray, Rorty, and others). Insofar as postmodernism occasions a retrieval of ancient sources, these contemporary sources will be brought into dialogue with Augustine, Irenaeus, Aquinas, and other resources. Drawing on the wisdom of established scholars in the field, the series will provide accessible introductions to postmodern thought with the specific aim of exploring its impact on ecclesial practice. The books are offered, one might say, as French lessons for the church.

Series Editor's Foreword

JAMES K. A. SMITH

When "postmodernism" is invoked outside the rather insulated confines of the academy, it is usually a shorthand for "anything goes," synonymous with unmitigated relativism and hermeneutic licentiousness. Granted, a lot that traffics under the banner of postmodernism seems to warrant this impression. Talk of the "death of the author" and the "play" of interpretation is often invoked for interpretive license. Indeed, interpretation is often seen as the root of the problem: postmodernism is perceived to be anything-goes relativism precisely because it assumes that "everything is a matter of interpretation." And we should note that there are both "left" and "right" versions of this. While some of us will worry that deconstructionists can make Milton or Paul mean anything they want, others worry when "interpretation" is a cover for redescribing torture as "enhanced interrogation techniques." In some ways we're all postmodernists now.

There is, then, an intertwining of postmodernism, interpretation, and the specter of relativism. And the stakes of this intertwining are raised in the contexts of communities of faith. For "peoples of the Book," whose way of life is shaped by texts, matters of interpretation are, in a way, matters of life and death. In fact, for Christians, many of the anxieties of hermeneutics are nothing new. Well before we were haunted by the specters of Derrida and Foucault, the Christian community grappled with the conflict of interpretations. One can see such conflicts embedded in the New Testament narrative itself. In Acts 15, for instance, we see a conflict of interpretations of "the law"—and we see a community grappling with interpretive difference within its midst. Despite a common mythology, the early church was not a hermeneutic paradise; rather, debates about what counts *as* the tradition have been integral to the Christian tradition. The early church was not a golden age of interpretive uniformity; rather, the catholic councils and creeds are the artifacts of a community facing up to the conflict of interpretations.

The Reformation perhaps unleashed this hermeneutic monster with a new intensity, and many of us live in its wake. If the Reformation was about anything, it was about being confronted anew by Scripture, wrestling with the text firsthand. It was nothing short of a Reformation of *reading*. And though the concern was to recover the gospel—to get back to *the* interpretation of salvation—the result, as we now know, was a proliferation of interpretations and the multiplication of interpretive communities. The irony is that, concurrent with this hermeneutic fragmentation, a specific hermeneutic doctrine arose regarding the perspicuity or "clarity" of Scripture. While medieval (read "Catholic") approaches to the Bible were portrayed as a morass of allegorical and imaginative acrobatics, the Reformers and their heirs championed the "plain sense" of Scripture. This basically amounted to the claim that, while others might *interpret* the Bible, we just *read* it, straight up, without any filters or biases or obfuscating meddling from ecclesiastical authorities. If we'd just stop interpreting and simply start reading, we'd arrive at the crystal-clear, objective truth of the matter. Thus the now-common refrain: Interpretation breeds relativism. Hermeneutics is the problem.

Whose Community? Which Interpretation? is a crisp, concise, provocative antidote to this common construal of the situation. And it comes from the pen of one of the masters. For two decades now I have prized and admired Merold Westphal's lucidity (not a term often associated with Continental philosophy!). He regularly weds erudition with a kind of folksy accessibility that is as entertaining as it is illuminating. Indeed, this book is essentially a "course in a box," a compact opportunity to learn from a master teacher. Crammed into this little book is a veritable curriculum on philosophical hermeneutics that gives us a peek into the background in figures like Schleiermacher and Dilthey, introduces us to critiques from Hirsch and Wolterstorff, and provides a core exposition of the great hermeneutic philosopher Hans-Georg Gadamer—all with a view to philosophical hermeneutics serving communities that read and pray and preach the Word.

I don't mean to suggest that Westphal is out to comfort all our fears and worries, to make interpretation safe and secure. Indeed, he will make the case for what he calls "relativist hermeneutics"—a label that's not going to thrill the purveyors of so-called absolute truth. But the burden of the book is to help us distinguish "anything goes" relativism from the relativity of finitude. One might say that Westphal is redeeming relativity and dependence, which seem to be the specific features of creaturehood. Along the way, he helps us navigate between "hermeneutical despair" and "hermeneutical arrogance." That, it seems to me, is a gift for the church.

Westphal can pull this off because these two worlds—philosophical hermeneutics and the church—come together in his thought. Or perhaps we could say that Westphal holds dual citizenship and is fluent in the language of both worlds. His project here is motivated by the conviction that the rigors of philosophical hermeneutics, when understood and appreciated, can actually help the church to be a faithful community of interpretation. Who could ask for more?

Preface

This book is intended for Christian theologians of three kinds: academic, pastoral, and lay. What they have in common is that they interpret the Bible and might do well to think about what is involved in such interpretation. By academic theologians I mean those whose interpretations are *written*; by pastoral theologians I mean those whose interpretations are *oral*; and by lay theologians I mean those whose interpretations take place in the *silence* of devotional reading. In publication, in preaching, and in private, personal reading, Christians interpret the Bible.

Since Christians are not isolated atoms but members of the body of Christ as the people of God, we can say that these three modes of interpretation are the ways in which the church interprets its Scripture. If the church misunderstands this vital task and privilege, it misunderstands its own identity, both communally and individually.

The first volume in this series, Jamie Smith's *Who's Afraid of Postmodernism?* bears the subtitle *Taking Derrida, Lyotard, and Foucault to Church*. This present volume might have had the subtitle *Taking Gadamer to Church*, for it is the hermeneutical theory of the German philosopher Hans-Georg Gadamer (1900–2002—yes, he lived that long) that I wish to present as an aid to thinking theologically about biblical hermeneutics ("hermeneutics" meaning the theory and practice of interpretation).

It is dangerous for Jerusalem (theology) to turn to Athens (philosophy) for guidance. The word of the cross does not conform to the wisdom of the world (1 Cor. 1:18–2:13). But there are two reasons why the risk is worth taking, especially when one is conscious of the danger. First, theologies that pride themselves on being free of contamination by philosophy are often, even usually, shaped by philosophical traditions that have become part of the culture to which these theologies belong and that operate without us being consciously aware of them. So an explicit reflection on philosophical issues in hermeneutics can be an aid to critical self-understanding. The point is not to be uncritical of some philosophical tradition (a genuine danger) but to be willing to be self-critical as theologians. Second, we just might learn something about interpretation that applies as much to biblical interpretation as to legal or literary interpretation.

Chapters 6 through 9 of this volume present Gadamer's theory. The first five chapters provide a preparation for "reading" him by providing some historical and contemporary context. The final three chapters explore the implications of Gadamerian hermeneutics within the context of the church, for if interpreting the Bible is in important respects like interpreting Shakespeare and the United States Constitution, it is in other important respects different. For example, the witness of the Holy Spirit, not only in attesting to the Bible as divine revelation but also in teaching us what it means, is a distinctively theological assumption that the church brings with it to the interpretation of Scripture. Theological hermeneutics will have other specific presuppositions that do not derive from philosophical hermeneutics and are not involved in interpreting Shakespeare or the Constitution.

Like others, such as Martin Heidegger and Paul Ricoeur, Gadamer insists that interpretation is never presuppositionless. We come with prejudices (pre-judgments) that shape our interpretations and that, in turn, are revised or even replaced in the course of interpretation. This is the hermeneutical circle in which presuppositions and interpretations mutually determine each other. But this means our interpretations are always relative to the presuppositions that we bring with us to the task of interpretation and that we have inherited and internalized from the traditions that have formed us. Unless we confuse ourselves—as tradition-bearing individuals and communities—with God, we will acknowledge a double relativity: our interpretations are relative to (conditioned by) the presuppositions we bring with us, and those presuppositions, as human, all too human, are themselves relative (penultimate, revisable, even replaceable) and not absolute.

One of the central arguments of this book is that such relativity is by no means the same as the relativism in which "anything goes." We are easily frightened by the specter of "anything goes," and there is no shortage of those willing to play on this fear in order to imply their own absoluteness. But there are three good reasons to resist this fear. First, from the relativity of our interpretations to the historical, cultural, and linguistic perspectives out of which they arise (as can be seen easily enough by looking at church history), it simply does not follow that "anything goes," that each viewpoint is as good as any other. Second, those who use "anything goes" as a fear tactic and as a defense against admitting their own relativity regularly fail to identify anyone who holds such a view. Not even Nietzsche, one of the most radical philosophical perspectivists, thinks that Christianity and Platonism are just as good as his own philosophy of the will to power. Third, there are good theological reasons to resist this fear. Under its influence, we end up thinking ourselves (our interpretations) to be absolute (at least in principle). But only God is absolute. Both because we are creatures and not the Creator and because we are fallen and not sinless, our vision is imperfect, at once finite and fallen.

We need not think that hermeneutical despair ("anything goes") and hermeneutical arrogance (we have "the" interpretation) are the only alternatives. We can acknowledge that we see and interpret "in a glass, darkly" or "in a mirror, dimly" and that we know "only in part" (1 Cor. 13:12), while ever seeking to understand and interpret better by combining the tools of scholarship with the virtues of humbly listening to the interpretations of others and above all to the Holy Spirit.

While this book is addressed to all Christians, including laity, I especially hope it will find its way to pastors and to readers in divinity schools and theological seminaries, where academic theologians and pastors in training properly engage not only in interpreting the Bible but also in reflecting on what this involves.

My thanks to Jamie Smith, for urging me to write such a treatise for his series, and to him, along with Ryan Weberling and especially my wife, Carol, for suggesting ways to make my argument clearer and more accessible.

1

Hermeneutics 101

No Interpretation Needed?

Interpretation or Intuition?

It may seem obvious that Christians interpret the Bible. Is not every devotional reading (silent), every sermon (spoken), and every commentary (written) an interpretation or a series of interpretations of a biblical text? Does not the history of Christian thought show that Christians in different times and places have interpreted and thus understood the Bible differently? Even at any given time and place, such as our own, is there not always a "conflict of interpretations"[1] between, among, and within various denominational and nondenominational traditions? So it seems obvious that Christians would be interested in hermeneutics, the theory of interpretation that is sometimes normative (how we ought to go about interpreting) and sometimes descriptive (what actually happens whenever we interpret).

But often enough the hermeneutical theory, if we may call it that, of lay believers, pastors, and academic theologians consists

1. The phrase is the title of a collection of essays by Paul Ricoeur, a major twentieth-century contributor to hermeneutical theory. The subtitle of that book is *Essays in Hermeneutics*, ed. Don Ihde (Evanston, IL: Northwestern University Press, 1974).

simply in denying that interpretation is necessary and unavoidable. We encounter this general attitude when we offer a viewpoint about, say, some controversial moral or political question to someone who (1) doesn't like it and (2) doesn't know how to refute it (perhaps deep down knowing that it is all too much on target) and so replies, "That's just your opinion." Similarly, an unwelcome interpretation of some biblical text may be greeted by the response, "Well, that might be *your* interpretation, but *my* Bible *clearly* says . . ." In other words, "You interpret; I just see what is plainly there." I am reminded of an ad for a new translation of the Bible billed as so accurate and so clear that the publishers could announce "NO INTERPRETA-TION NEEDED."[2] The ad promotes "the revolutionary translation that allows you to immediately understand exactly what the original writers meant." But, of course, this "immediacy" is mediated by this particular translation, one among many, each of which interprets the original text[3] a bit differently from the others.

This "no interpretation needed" doctrine says that interpretation is accidental and unfortunate, that it can and should be avoided whenever possible. Often unnoticed is that this theory is itself an interpretation of interpretation and that it belongs to a long-standing philosophical tradition that stretches from certain strands in Plato's thought well into the twentieth century. This tradition is called "naive realism" in one of its forms. It is called naive both descriptively, because it is easily taken by a common-sense perspective without philosophical reflection, and normatively, because it is taken to be indefensible on careful philosophical reflection. Before looking into why this interpretation of interpretation might deserve to be called naive in this second sense, let us first try to be clear about *what* it asserts and *why*.

Realism begins as the claim that the world (the real) is "out there" and is what it is independent of whether or what we might think about it. But since, in spite of appearances, no one actually denies this, if realism is to be a claim worthy of defending or denying, it must say more, and it does. It is the further claim that we can (at least sometimes) know reality just as it is, independent of our judgments about it. In other words, our thoughts or judgments about the world correspond to it,

    2. See James K. A. Smith, *The Fall of Interpretation: Philosophical Foundations for a Creational Hermeneutic* (Downers Grove, IL: InterVarsity, 2000), 39. Jamie Smith, the editor of the present series, first called this ad to my attention years ago at a conference on biblical hermeneutics, and I have often had occasion to recall it.
    3. More precisely, the latest scholarly version of the original text.

perfectly mirror it.[4] It is because Kant, who affirms the first claim, denies the second claim that he is the paradigmatic antirealist. He insists that we don't know the "thing in itself," the world as it truly is, but only the world as it appears to human—all too human—understanding. We don't apprehend it *directly* but only as *mediated* through the forms and categories we bring with us to experience.[5] In other words, the human mind is a kind of receiving apparatus, like a black and white TV set, that conditions the way in which what is "out there" appears. Thus the world *as we see it* is partly the result of the way the real gives itself to us (as passive, receptive) and partly the result of the way we take it (as active, spontaneous). Like the Gestalt psychologist, Kant does not suggest that we are aware of our contributing role, that our "taking" is conscious or voluntary, much less deliberate. It happens, so to speak, behind our backs.

Incidentally, although scholars usually ignore this fact, Kant regularly identifies appearances as the way we see the world and the "thing in itself" as the way God sees the world.[6] Things really are the way the divine mind knows them to be. So theists, who have good reason not to identify our finite, creaturely understanding of reality with God's infinite, creative knowledge, have a sound theological reason for being Kantian antirealists. Our thoughts are not God's thoughts (divine wisdom) any more than our ways are God's ways (divine holiness, mercy, and love).

> For as the heavens are higher than the earth,
>   so are my ways higher than your ways
>   and my thoughts than your thoughts. (Isa. 55:9)

Naive realists, including the "no interpretation needed" school, who may never have heard of Kant or of antirealism, deny, at least implicitly, the inevitability of such mediation. They affirm a direct seeing that simply mirrors what is there without in any way affect-

---

4. The image in an imperfect mirror, like the funny mirror at the circus, fails to correspond to its object.

5. Kant calls these elements a priori. Because we bring them with us to experience, they are in place prior to any particular experience in which the real gives itself to us, and they function as "the conditions of possible experience." In other words, the a priori compels the real to appear in a certain way. See Kant's *Critique of Pure Reason*.

6. See Merold Westphal, "In Defense of the Thing in Itself," *Kant-Studien* 59, no. 1 (1968): 118–41.

ing what is seen *as it is seen.* Plato expresses this view in connection with the philosopher's apprehension of the forms—the purely intelligible structures that are the highest, indeed the only, objects of genuine knowledge—when he speaks of contemplating "things by themselves with the soul by itself."[7]

In speaking of this direct, unmediated rendezvous of subject and object (of whatever sort), philosophers view the object as *immediately given* or *immediately present.* The claim to *immediacy* is the claim that the object is given to the subject without any mediating (contaminating, distorting) input from the subject, be it the lens through which the object is seen, the perspective from which the object is seen, or the presupposition in terms of which the object is seen, all of which might vary from one observer to another or from one community of observers to another.

Common sense doesn't talk about immediacy, presence, or givenness. But it does claim to "just see" its objects, free of bias, prejudice, and presuppositions (at least sometimes). We can call this "just seeing" intuition. When the naive-realist view of knowledge and understanding is applied to reading texts, such as the Bible, it becomes the claim that we can "just see" what the text means, that intuition can and should be all we need. In other words, "no interpretation needed." The object, in this case the meaning of the text, presents itself clearly and directly to my reading. To interpret would be to interject some subjective bias or prejudice (pre-judgment) into the process. Thus the response, "Well, that might be your interpretation, but *my* Bible *clearly* says . . ." In other words, "You interpret (and thereby misunderstand), but I intuit, seeing directly, clearly, and without distortion."

Why Seek to Avoid Interpretation?

Let us turn to the question of motivation. Why would anyone want to hold to the hermeneutical version of naive realism? Let us dismiss (but not too quickly) the suspicion that this view is attractive because it makes it so easy to say: "I am (we are) right, and all who

---

7. *Phaedo* 66e. For Plato this pure and uncontaminated knowledge of pure and uncontaminated reality (the thing in itself) is possible only insofar as the soul has freed itself from the body, that is, its *senses* and *desires.* For modern philosophy, as a theme and variation on Descartes, genuine knowledge occurs when thought is no longer shaped by *tradition.*

disagree are wrong, and not merely wrong but wrong because of bias or prejudice."[8]

There are more respectable reasons, two of which immediately come to the fore: the desire to preserve truth as correspondence and the desire to preserve objectivity, a closely related notion, in our reading, preaching, and commenting. So far as truth is concerned, the hermeneutical question is not whether what the text says corresponds to or perfectly mirrors the real; it is rather whether what the reader, preacher, or commentator says corresponds to what the text says. This is especially important if we take the Bible to be the Word of God that as such again and again becomes the Word of God for us as we read it for ourselves or pay attention to its exposition by the preacher or commentator. But if, according to the Kantian interpretation of interpretation, what we find in the text is a mixture of what is there and the (human, all too human) lens through which we read and by which the text is mediated to us, is the voice we hear divine or merely human? The hermeneutics of immediacy is not the only way to preserve correspondence between what the text says and what we take it to say, but it is probably the simplest.

Closely related to the notion of truth as correspondence is the notion of objectivity. For the sake of truth as opposed to mere opinion ("That's just your opinion"), it may seem that the contingent and particular factors that make one knower or knowing community different from others should be filtered out as subjective and distorting. Since Plato, mathematics, which is highly immune to subjective interpretations, has been a paradigm—if not the paradigm—for truth as objectivity. We should all get the same answer to the question "What is the square root of sixteen?"[9]

If we ask what are the contingent and particular factors that need to be filtered out—the a prioris, the lenses, the presuppositions, the receiving apparatuses that might contaminate our readings and produce misunderstanding—one of the most conspicuous candidates would be the traditions within which the Bible is read and expounded. The rich diversity of readings of the Bible that make up Christian history

8. Or perhaps, "We are the people, and wisdom will die with us" (see Job 12:2). This *attitude* might be taken to be the *formal* definition of fundamentalism, whether political or theological, whether of the left (liberal) or the right (conservative).

9. This is an interesting example, because there are two right answers, not just one, and the student capable of answering "four" might not be able to give the answer "negative four."

are not, for the most part, the result of individual idiosyncrasy but of traditions that have developed and are passed on and shared by communities and generations. The desert fathers, the Geneva Calvinists, the American slaves, and today's Amish belong to different traditions of interpretation, as do the two sides of the debate within the Episcopal Church (and others) over homosexuality.

This is precisely a powerful motivation to privilege intuition over interpretation, for the latter seems linked to the notion (or rather reality) of different traditions, and if interpretation is relative to the tradition in which it occurs, the specter of relativism haunts us. If the meaning derived is a product both of the text and of the tradition within which the text is read, we arrive at a familiar question: what happens to truth and to the voice of God if every understanding of the Bible is relative to some human, all too human, tradition of interpretation? Once again, the appeal to intuition, to "just seeing" what the Bible says, is not the only way to attempt to avoid relativism, but it is quick and clean, if it can be sustained.

Can Interpretation Be Avoided?

But can the appeal to intuition be sustained? The case for "just seeing" is not easy to make, and the naive realism inherent in the "no interpretation needed" viewpoint may prove to be naive in the second, pejorative sense given above. As we have just seen, however briefly, the whole idea that some construals are subjective interpretations while others are objective intuitions is itself a particular (contested) tradition within philosophy. It is ironic that proponents of theologies that like to think of themselves as innocent of (uncontaminated by) philosophical prejudices (pre-judgments, presuppositions) so easily make themselves heirs of this tradition. It looks as if this hermeneutics, this interpretation of interpretation, is itself relative to the presuppositions of a particular philosophical tradition.

To make matters worse, in a variety of normative areas, including ethics, politics, and theology, individuals and communities appeal to intuitions, to what we've been calling "just seeings," that are as divergent as the traditions from which they are an attempt to flee. There is a "conflict of intuition" just as much as there is a "conflict of interpretation." And it may be that tradition is at work in the one case as much as it is in the other. Take racial bias as an example. If I have grown up in a racist community and been effectively socialized into it, I will "just see" that people who belong to a particular racial or ethnic group are morally and intellectually inferior to me and my kind, possibly to the degree of being only semihuman. Quite possibly I will "just see" that the Bible supports my view of the matter. My receiving apparatus has been so formed by a living and effective tradition that the people in question cannot appear to me otherwise (unless and until I am resocialized out of this community of interpretation and into another). We too easily deceive ourselves on this point. What I "just see" as a construal that "just sees" its object with a pure immediacy of intuition may be an interpretation richly mediated by a tradition that is alive and well both in my community and in my own thinking.

While it is easy to show that we can be mistaken in taking a particular seeing to be a "just seeing," it is harder, if not impossible, to show that no one ever has intuitions that are genuinely immediate. But perhaps the rush to immediacy can be slowed down and (by anticipation) the general fear of relativity somewhat assuaged if we look at some models where the plurality of viewpoints is not a compromise of truth and objectivity.

Consider the following figure (fig. 1.1).

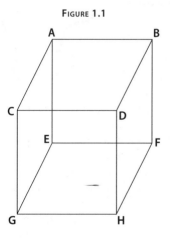

FIGURE 1.1

We are told it is the schema of a box with five cardboard sides and an open top. Whenever I draw this figure I see ABDC as the open top. This construal comes so naturally that it seems immediate, and experientially speaking, it is. I "just see" it that way. But then I remember that there is another way to see it. It takes some time and some work, but eventually I see ABFE as the open top. In the first case, I am slightly to the right of the box and can see its right-hand side from the outside, but not the left-hand side. In the second case, I am slightly to the left of the box and can see the left-hand side from the outside, but not the right-hand side. But neither of these seeings is right in the way that makes the other wrong. Note that even though there are two correct answers to the question "Where is the open top?" it does not mean that every answer is correct. ACGE, CDHG, EFHG, and BDHF could all be seen as open sides, but not as the open top.

Or consider the famous duck-rabbit that Wittgenstein borrows from Jastrow (fig. 1.2).[10]

Figure 1.2

If I see the critter as looking to the left, I see it as a duck. But if I see it as looking slightly up and to the right, I see it as a rabbit. Here again, neither seeing is *the* right one. But, of course, it would be quite wrong to say the figure is a moose or a spider.[11]

These two figures are sufficiently indeterminate to accommodate more than one seeing as correct without permitting the "anything goes" relativism that is conjured up as a bogeyman at the first hint that human understanding might be relative to human conditions.

10. In speaking of examples of this kind, Ludwig Wittgenstein writes, "So we interpret it, and *see* it as we *interpret* it" (*Philosophical Investigations*, trans. G. E. M. Anscombe [Oxford: Blackwell, 1958], 193–94).

11. Just as it would be wrong to say that the square root of sixteen is five. See note 9 of this chapter.

The question that arises is whether certain kinds of texts, including
biblical texts, are like this.

Another possibility is suggested by the following poem:

> There were six men of Hindustan,
>   to learning much inclined,
> Who went to see an elephant,
>   though all of them were blind,
> That each by observation
>   might satisfy his mind.
>
> The first approached the elephant,
>   and happening to fall
> Against his broad and sturdy side,
>   at once began to bawl,
> "This mystery of an elephant
>   is very like a wall."
>
> The second, feeling of the tusk,
>   cried, "Ho, what have we here,
> So very round and smooth and sharp?
>   To me 'tis mighty clear,
> This wonder of an elephant
>   is very like a spear."
>
> The third approached the elephant,
>   and happening to take
> The squirming trunk within his hands,
>   thus boldly up and spake,
> "I see," quoth he,
>   "the elephant is very like a snake."
>
> The fourth reached out an eager hand,
>   and felt above the knee,
> "What this most wondrous beast
>   is like is very plain," said he,
> "'Tis clear enough the elephant is very like a tree."
>
> The fifth who chanced to touch the ear
>   said, "E'en the blindest man
> Can tell what this resembles most;
>   deny the fact who can;
> This marvel of an elephant is very like a fan."

The sixth no sooner had begun
    about the beast to grope,
Than seizing on the swinging tail
    that fell within his scope;
"I see," said he, "the elephant is very like a rope."

So six blind men of Hindustan
    disputed loud and long,
Each in his own opinion
    exceeding stiff and strong;
Though each was partly in the right,
    they all were in the wrong![12]

Here the multiplicity of interpretations stems not from the in-determinacy of the object but from the way it exceeds the ability of any limited perspective to grasp it in its totality. Each man's perspective (tradition?) enabled him to grasp an aspect of the elephant that the others failed to grasp. So each was "partly in the right" as a perspective without which the truth about the elephant could not be told. But "all were in the wrong" because they took their partial grasp for the whole. Hence the quarrel, which might easily have turned violent if the elephant were considered sacred. It is precisely the inability of human understanding to grasp reality in its totality that led Kant to downgrade human understanding in comparison with divine.

Here the hermeneutical question arises whether some texts, including the biblical texts, are like the elephant: rich enough to *require*, not merely to *permit*, a multitude of different readings just because human readings are always partial and perspectival and because no single reading is able to capture and express the overflow of meaning these texts contain. We think this way about Shakespeare. Why not think this way about the Bible? Once again the possibility of necessary multiplicity does not open the door to just anything. None of the six blind men had warrant to say the elephant was like a keyboard or a file cabinet.

---

12. This poem is found at various sites on the Internet without attribution or copyright.

2

Hermeneutics 102

A Little Historical Background

Romantic Hermeneutics: Deregionalization and the Hermeneutical Circle

Philosophical hermeneutics is general reflection on the nature of interpretation. Among the most influential interpretations of interpretation in the twentieth century are those of Martin Heidegger, Hans-Georg Gadamer, and Paul Ricoeur. Gadamer will be our primary protagonist in subsequent chapters, but the work of all three needs to be seen against the background of nineteenth-century developments, especially the hermeneutics of Friedrich Schleiermacher and Wilhelm Dilthey.[1] This is not to suggest that the rich tradition of premodern (pre-Enlightenment) theological hermeneutics is no longer of interest. Far from it![2] It is only to

1. For a more detailed account of this history, see Merold Westphal, *Overcoming Onto-theology: Toward a Postmodern Christian Faith* (New York: Fordham University Press, 2001), chaps. 8 and 6, in that order.
2. See, e.g., Jens Zimmermann, *Recovering Theological Hermeneutics: An Incarnational-Trinitarian Theory of Interpretation* (Grand Rapids: Baker Academic, 2004),

choose to begin our exploration of Gadamer and friends with a look at their most immediate predecessors.

In Schleiermacher's day there were three academic disciplines in which interpretation was especially important: law, classical philology (what we would call literary criticism), and theology. Students were taught how to interpret the law, the classics, and the Bible, respectively. In what Ricoeur has called the *deregionalization* of hermeneutics,[3] Schleiermacher set out to develop a general hermeneutics that would apply to culturally significant texts regardless of their subject matter.[4] He sought to identify the general features of interpretation that were *common to* rather than *distinctive of* the various disciplines. Especially for this reason, and not only because it has roots in biblical interpretation, philosophical hermeneutics has been and should be of interest to theology, whether biblical interpretation is personal, pastoral, or scholarly.[5]

A second distinctive feature of Schleiermacher's theory is the hermeneutical circle. It is the notion that the parts always have to be interpreted in terms of the whole—and vice versa. There are two major circles for Schleiermacher: one is grammatical-linguistic, the other is psychological. In the first case, the movement from part to ever-larger whole goes from sentence (1) to text (this pericope, this chapter, this book), (2) to genre (or textual tradition), (3) to the whole language shared by the author and original readers, (4) and finally to the history of human language. In the second case, one moves from this work of the author (1) to the author's entire body of writing, (2) to the author's whole life as known to us from other sources, (3) and finally to what we know of the nation and era to which the author belongs. The first circle focuses on the text, the second on the author.

---

for theological hermeneutics in the Reformation traditions and the claim that contemporary philosophical hermeneutics should pay greater attention to these traditions.

3. Paul Ricoeur, *Hermeneutics and the Human Sciences: Essays on Language, Action, and Interpretation*, trans. John B. Thompson (New York: Cambridge University Press, 1981), 44. Heidegger represents a *radicalization* of hermeneutics in that for him interpretation is not something we sometimes do but rather something that becomes fundamental to who we *are* and is characteristic of *all* modes of knowing, not just textual interpretation. Or, to put it differently, the whole of reality becomes a text to be interpreted. See Westphal, *Overcoming Onto-theology*, chap. 3.

4. He had little interest in grocery lists or want ads.

5. Cf. the silent, spoken, or written triad of chap. 1.

The relation between whole and part is circular in that each is interpreted in light of the other; interpretation is a reciprocal interaction in which neither variable is independent of the other. The interpretation of the parts is guided by and revised in light of the whole, but my view of the whole is guided by and revised in light of my reading of the parts. Consider, for example, *Gulliver's Travels*. Knowing nothing about it, I pick it up at my local library because I love travelogs, and I try to read it in the light of this projection (anticipation) of the whole. This doesn't work too well, and I soon replace my assumption about the book's genre with a new one: this is children's fiction. Guided by my new sense of the whole, I find the parts to make more sense than before, but they remain somewhat recalcitrant. What's the point of this or that aspect of the text? If I have enough background knowledge or get some outside help, I may formulate a third hypothesis about the whole: this is political satire in the guise of kiddy lit. Now the parts begin to make more sense but *only to the degree that I know something about the author and his sociopolitical context*. This move from the purely textual to the biographical-historical indicates that the two major circles described by Schleiermacher together form a hermeneutically circular whole. We interpret the text in light of the person, though much of what we know about the person we learn only from the text.

Romantic Hermeneutics: Psychologism and Objectivism

These two features of "romantic" hermeneutics—deregionalization and the hermeneutical circle—are widely shared in the philosophical hermeneutics of the twentieth century. But the next two features are widely challenged. The third crucial characteristic of "romantic" hermeneutics is its *psychologism*. It begins with the assumption that language is primarily to be understood as the outer expression of the inner psychic life. This hermeneutics is often labeled "romantic" because it shares this expressivism with the wider cultural traditions called romanticism.[6] The goal of interpretation, then, is to reverse

6. See Charles Taylor, *Hegel and Modern Society* (New York: Cambridge University Press, 1979), 1–3. This theme is central to the latter portions of Taylor's *Sources of the Self: The Making of the Modern Identity* (Cambridge, MA: Harvard University Press, 1989), chaps. 21–25.

the process of writing, to work back from the outer expression to the inner experience, to reconstruct, re-create, refeel, reexperience, relive that inner experience. Schleiermacher tells us that "every act of understanding is the reverse side of an act of speaking, and one must grasp the thinking that underlies a given statement." Or again, one "must be able to step out of one's own frame of mind into that of the author." Or still again, "Before the art of hermeneutics can be practiced, the interpreter must put himself both objectively and subjectively in the position of the author."[7]

The same psychologism comes to light when Dilthey describes the goal of interpretation as "to feel the states of mind of others." It is a "congenial empathetic projection into the soul of other peoples and ages" and "the intuitive grasp of the creative process by which a literary work comes into being." Dilthey would be glad to hear of the orchestra conductors who say they sometimes feel as if they were composing the piece as they conduct it. The interpreter "tentatively [remember the hermeneutic circle] projects his own sense of life into another historical milieu . . . thus making possible within himself a re-creation of an alien form of life." In other words, "We therefore call understanding that process by which we recognize, behind signs given to our senses, that psychic reality of which they are the expression."[8] Ricoeur says much the same when he describes interpretation as "sympathetic re-enactment in imagination" or a "re-enactment in sympathetic imagination."[9]

In addition to notions of empathy, sympathy, and projection of oneself into the experience and life of others, the goal it sets for interpretation is a crucial feature of this psychologism. Schleiermacher is quite clear: "By leading the interpreter to transfer himself, so to speak, into the author, the divinatory method seeks to gain an immediate comprehension *of the author as an individual*."[10]

7. Friedrich Schleiermacher, *Hermeneutics: The Handwritten Manuscripts*, ed. Heinz Kimmerle, trans. James Duke and Jack Forstman (Missoula, MT: Scholars Press, 1977), 97, 42, 113.

8. Wilhelm Dilthey, "The Rise of Hermeneutics," in *Selected Works*, vol. 4, *Hermeneutics and the Study of History*, ed. Rudolf A. Makkreel and Frithjof Rodi (Princeton, NJ: Princeton University Press, 1996), 235, 246, 249, and 236.

9. Paul Ricoeur, *The Symbolism of Evil*, trans. Emerson Buchanan (New York: Harper & Row, 1967), 3, 19. Ricoeur's later hermeneutical theory abandons this psychologism. See, e.g., *Interpretation Theory: Discourse and the Surplus of Meaning* (Fort Worth: Texas Christian University Press, 1976), 29–32.

10. Schleiermacher, *Hermeneutics*, 150; emphasis added.

It is especially for this reason that Gadamer and (later) Ricoeur will distance themselves from the psychologism of "romantic" hermeneutics. Occasionally we read a text to learn about its author, but more typically we read to learn about the subject matter (*Sache*) of the text, the natural, human, or divine realities the text is about.[11] We don't normally read Shakespeare to learn about William (or whoever wrote those wonderful plays) but to learn about human nature, its possibilities and its pitfalls. Similarly, we read Wordsworth, most of the time, not to learn about his inner life but to learn (among other things) alternatives to the modern scientific objectification of nature. And we read Paul to learn (among other things) about justification, baptism, and what it means to be "in Christ." To be sure, we learn something about Paul from reading the Corinthian epistles, and more than we ever wanted to know about the Corinthian Christians; but normally we read and interpret these texts not to learn what it was like to be Paul but to learn what Paul *had* to say on a variety of topics—and what God *has* to say to us today through what Paul wrote.

A fourth and final feature of "romantic" hermeneutics is its objectivism. Dilthey is especially insistent that interpretation be "*scientific*" so that its findings may be "objective" and rise to the level of "universal validity."[12] The prestige and power of the natural sciences seem to suggest that rational respectability requires that the disciplines that relate to distinctly human meaning (*Geisteswissenschaften*, humanities, human sciences) must aspire to a comparable objectivity, especially against the possibility of some sort of historical relativism. Dilthey affirms the value of historical consciousness but fears that our embeddedness within historically particular and contingent worldviews and traditions implies "the relativity of every kind of human apprehension of the totality of things"—the whole of the hermeneutical circle. In other words, he fears that our interpretations will be relative to presuppositions that are not universally shared and are thus subjective. It matters not whether these are shared by whole cultures or epochs so long as they remain particular and not universal. So he asks, "But where are the means to overcome the anarchy

11. Schleiermacher sometimes talks this way himself, so while at times he seems to espouse psychologism, at other times he talks as if getting inside the author is not in itself the goal but only a means to seeing *the world* through the author's eyes. See Westphal, *Overcoming Onto-theology*, 115–16.

12. Dilthey, "Rise of Hermeneutics," 235–38.

of opinions that then threatens to befall us?"[13] He fears a "different strokes for different folks" philosophy in which truth will be lost in a sea of opinions. A whole discipline, known as the sociology of knowledge, has arisen to deal with this "vertigo of relativity."[14]

This question haunts hermeneutics to this day. Dilthey's answer is method, which he understands primarily in terms of rules. Interpretation can and must be objective in the manner of the sciences; it must avoid the subjectivity of particular perspectives, which by their very nature vary from person to person, from community to community, and from tradition to tradition. It can achieve this goal only if it is the application of rules to the texts in question.[15] So he gives us these two definitions: "Such rule-guided understanding of fixed and relatively permanent objectifications of life [note the expressivism here] is what we call exegesis or interpretation." Hermeneutics is the theory of the rules for interpreting written monuments.[16] Interpretation is rule-governed understanding; hermeneutics legislates and adjudicates the rules.

Schleiermacher more often speaks of interpretation as an art than as a science. But he also aspires to objectivity through method. In a passage cited above he speaks of "the divinatory method," but divination is most definitely not his method. By divination he means what was called intuition in our previous chapter, and thus he speaks of "immediate comprehension." But for him, that is not so much the method as the goal of his method. It is something that arises "suddenly"[17] like a Gestalt switch when the "penny drops" or the "light dawns" and we "just see" what the text means. But this result, which is always provisional and subject to revision, is the result of painstaking, methodical labor in which the interpreter (1) works back and forth from smaller parts to a larger whole within the grammatical-linguistic circle, (2) does the same within the psy-

13. Dilthey, "Reminiscences on Historical Studies at the University of Berlin," in *Hermeneutics and the Study of History*, 389.

14. See Peter L. Berger and Thomas Luckmann, *The Social Construction of Reality: A Treatise in the Sociology of Knowledge* (Garden City, NY: Doubleday, 1966), 5; Peter Berger, *A Rumor of Angels: Modern Society and the Rediscovery of the Supernatural* (Garden City, NY: Doubleday, 1970), 32.

15. Question for Dilthey: don't different communities and traditions have different rules for the interpretation of legal, literary, and scriptural texts?

16. Dilthey, "Rise of Hermeneutics," 237–38.

17. Schleiermacher, *Hermeneutics*, 198.

chological-historical circle, and (3) works back and forth within the circle formed by these two in relation to each other. In other words, divinatory intuition is an immediacy that is itself highly mediated. Just as the intuitions of racial bias are mediated by socialization into a world that is itself mediated by a variety of historical and psychological developments, so too are hermeneutical intuitions mediated by scholarly work under the guidance of a method. The former mediation is by means of a particular and contingent social formation, while the latter is supposed to filter out precisely such subjective factors. The difference between that socialization and this scholarly work is that the latter is intended to let the text speak for itself, free from subjective distortions, whether personal and psychological or cultural and sociohistorical. The hermeneutical circle signifies that we will always approach a text with presuppositions or preunderstandings that guide our readings. But these are understood to be provisional, like hypotheses in the quantitative-experimental sciences. They are to be rigorously tested by means of methodical procedures meant to show whether the available evidence supports them. The ideal is to start subjectively but end objectively.

In the last chapter we saw the appeal to sheer immediacy expressed in the "no interpretation needed" view as an allergic reaction to the specter of relativism. Now we can see the appeal to method as a second way of responding to that perceived threat. Romantic hermeneutics recognizes the moment of immediacy in interpretation, the moment when we "just see" what the text means. But, fully aware of the "conflict of intuitions," it does not stake its claim to objectivity on these all-too-subjective experiences. (Remember the racist who "just sees" others to be inferior and not worthy of equal respect.) Rather, it appeals to method, to rule-governed discovery and testing procedures, to purify interpretation from subjective contamination and to lead it to universal validity, where all interpreters get the same (presumably right) answer to the question: what does this text mean? Methodical hermeneutics is the strict teacher who maintains order in a classroom that otherwise would degenerate into a chaos of spit-ball throwing, pea shooting, hair pulling, and name calling.

The hermeneutics of Gadamer will leave behind these last two features of "romantic" hermeneutics. He will abandon its psychologism because (1) he does not take the expression of inner experience

to be the primary function of language,[18] (2) accordingly, he takes
the goal of interpretation in nonbiographical contexts to be to understand what the author is saying about some important subject
matter rather than what it is like to be that author, and (3) he does
not think the author has the ability to impose meaning unilaterally
on the text.

Gadamer will also part company with the objectivism of "romantic" hermeneutics, especially that of Dilthey in his fear of relativism. He doesn't think that there is a method or set of rules that
can extricate us from the hermeneutical circle, which means that
our understanding will always be relative to the currently operative
presuppositions that shape our interpretations. Any method or rules
we adopt will themselves be interpretations of how we should proceed and are themselves caught up in one or another hermeneutical
circle. It is nice to have a method or a set of rules to function as the
criterion of interpretation. But the question can always be asked:
by what criteria are these criteria justified?

In Gadamerian hermeneutics we will encounter a third response
to the question of relativism. But there is a prior consideration.

---

18. Though it might be the purpose of, say, confessional poetry.

3

Against Romantic Hermeneutics

Away from Psychologism

The hermeneutic tradition whose founding fathers are Heidegger, Gadamer, and Ricoeur has no neat name. So I will bite the bullet and give it a name, an ugly name that will scare some readers: relativist hermeneutics. This trio shares the following interpretation of the hermeneutical circle: First, we are always somewhere (socially, culturally, historically, linguistically) and never nowhere when we interpret. Interpretation is never without presuppositions. It is always relative to the particular and contingent "location" of the interpreter. Of course, we can always seek, as individuals or communities, to become aware of our presuppositions and to subject them to scrutiny and critique. But we are always somewhere and *never* nowhere in doing this, that is, evaluating a tradition of interpretation to which we belong in the light of some other tradition to which we also belong or to which we have been willing to listen seriously.

So, second, we never escape from the hermeneutical circularity in which we always find ourselves already located. Of course, we can move from one circle to another, like the racist who becomes converted to one of the various language games of equal respect, but we never escape all somewhere to arrive at nowhere. We are like snakes that slough off one skin only to inhabit another.

Because Heidegger expands the notion of interpretation well beyond the realm of text interpretation,[1] he will be of less interest to us. Our focus will be on Gadamer and Ricoeur, especially the former. They retain the "deregionalization" of hermeneutics and seek a *general* theory of textual interpretation, and they retain the notion of the hermeneutical circle, as just noted. But they repudiate both the psychologism and, in their understanding of the hermeneutical circle, the objectivism of "romantic" hermeneutics. Before turning to the rejection of objectivism, we need to look at the rejection of psychologism, which helpfully prepares the way for the former; and before turning directly to Gadamer and Ricoeur, it might be helpful to present a few reasons to look at Nick Wolterstorff's repudiation of hermeneutical psychologism, grounded in speech act theory rather than Heideggerian phenomenology. One reason is the conceptual clarification it provides. Another reason is that it is an overtly theological hermeneutics and is a good example of why philosophical (deregionalized) and theological hermeneutics can and should converse with each other.

Speech Act Theory

First, a brief introduction to speech act theory. It traces its origins to a book by J. L. Austin with the interesting title, *How to Do Things with Words*.[2] When we use language, we speak or write, that is, we utter or inscribe sentences. But Austin asks what it is we *do* when we do this. Philosophers often talk as if the only thing we do is make assertions. But Austin points out that we do a wide variety of other things as well. We offer comfort; we ask questions; we make requests; we make promises; we express disapproval by means of sarcasm or irony; and so forth. When, under the proper circumstances, I say "I do," I do several things with words at once. I make a solemn promise; I change my marital status; I delight (or perhaps disappoint) my family. Austin calls these speech acts "performatives" because in uttering a short sentence I also perform these other acts.

1. See chap. 2, note 3.
2. J. L. Austin, *How to Do Things with Words* (Oxford: Claredon, 1962).

There are several things to notice about speech acts:

- Like other actions, they are subject to moral and legal norms. I ought not to utter "I do" if I do not intend to keep the solemn promise made thereby. I ought not to change my marital status with this person to "married" if I am already married to someone else. I ought not to disappoint my family out of sheer malice.
- Speech acts are subject to norms in another way. Only under the right circumstances, defined by rules of law or custom, do they count as the intended performance. I don't change my marital status (at least in the eyes of the state and the church) if I say "I take you to be my wife" while the two of us are alone on the beach or if I am already married. Nor have I performed the act of pardoning a prisoner if I say, "I pardon you," but am not the governor or president but only a fellow gang member.
- For the speech acts just cited, these norms are not those of truth or falsity but rather those of appropriateness in terms of such considerations as sincerity and authority. They involve the duties and rights of speakers. We can ask, "Do you really mean it?" and "Do you have the authority to do that?" but it would be a misunderstanding to ask, "Is that true or false?"
- This is because not all speech acts are assertions. But assertions can also be seen as performatives. In uttering or inscribing I am doing something else: I am making an assertion. Questions of sincerity and authority are also appropriate here. Do you really believe that? Do you have the right to tell us that? But in this case questions of truth or falsity are also appropriate.[7]

Here ends the very short course on speech act theory. Yes, there will be a quiz.

A Hermeneutics of Divine Discourse

Drawing on speech act theory, Nicholas Wolterstorff develops a specifically theological hermeneutics in a splendid book titled *Divine Discourse: Philosophical Reflections on the Claim That God*

Speaks.[3] He wants speech act theory to illuminate the claim that the Bible *is* the Word of God and that the Bible *becomes* the Word of God again and again in various times and places. When we read the Bible or hear it proclaimed in preaching, we are addressed and, above and beyond any human speaker or writer who may be involved, it is God by whom we are addressed.

Wolterstorff seeks to expound and defend a hermeneutics of "authorial discourse interpretation" that will involve the abandonment of hermeneutical psychologism. He prepares the way with three preliminary claims. First, God speaks. God performs speech acts. Of course God does not have a physical tongue or hand with which to utter or inscribe. But it is not a mere metaphor to say that God engages in discourse, which is understood as the event in which someone says something about something to someone. God is a someone who can do just that. This is a metaphysical claim of the first importance. Without it, "God" or "the sacred" becomes some sort of impersonal force or ideal. For biblical faith, God must be a truly personal agent, and a God not personal enough to speak would not seem to be personal enough to love. In short, such a God would not be the God of the Bible. To call the Bible the Word of God would be to engage in mere metaphor, as when the poet tells us that the west wind beckons him up and away.

Second, as we have just seen, not all speech acts are assertions. Just as philosophers often talk as if they were, so theologians often talk as if divine discourse consists primarily in assertions whose purpose is revelation, or, to be more precise, self-revelation. Wolterstorff challenges this assumption in a chapter with the provocative title, "Speaking Is Not Revealing." He does not deny that sometimes the primary purpose of a speech act is self-revelation, as when I say, "I'm tired" or "I've got an ache in my left knee" or "I love you." Nor does he deny that in doing other things with words we often also, but secondarily, reveal something about ourselves. The request or command, "Turn up the heat," normally reveals that I am chilly. Wolterstorff's point is rather that speaking does not necessarily have self-revelation as its primary function for either human or divine speakers. In the latter case, he suggests that divine discourse com-

---

3. Nicholas Wolterstorff, *Divine Discourse: Philosophical Reflections on the Claim That God Speaks* (New York: Cambridge University Press, 1995). See Merold Westphal, "On Reading God the Author," *Religious Studies* 37 (2001): 271–91.

ing to us in and through the Bible more typically has the form of promises or commands (*just the speech acts necessary for covenantal relationships*), speech acts that may presuppose assertions of various sorts but that are not themselves assertions, much less assertions about God as speaker.

Third, when God spoke long ago "in many and various ways by the prophets" (Heb. 1:1), human tongues and hands were put to use. The Bible consists of inscriptions made by human hands, often containing a record of utterances made with human tongues. To say that the Bible is nevertheless the Word of God is to invoke the notion of double discourse. The idea is quite simple. Sometimes one person performs speech acts by means of the utterances or inscriptions of another. Citing the account of Augustine's conversion in *Confessions* 8.12, Wolterstorff calls attention to three cases of double discourse. Here Augustine writes of hearing a child repeating the injunction "*tolle lege, tolle lege*" (take and read) and taking this to be a command addressed to him by God. He remembers how Antony was converted when he entered a church and heard a reading from Matthew 19:21, "Go home and sell all that belongs to you. Give it to the poor."[4] Antony understood it to be God speaking to him by means of a human voice that was reading what a human hand had written. Similarly, Augustine himself promptly reads from Romans 13:13–14, "Not in reveling and drunkenness . . . Rather, arm yourselves with the Lord Jesus Christ." In a text dictated by Paul, inscribed by his amanuensis, copied by who knows how many others, eventually translated into Latin, and again copied numerous times, Augustine hears the voice of God addressing him directly and personally. In these cases the human voice that is heard and the text that is read become the bearers of the very voice of God. One could almost speak here of a *transubstantiation*. An empirical reality within the created world does not merely point beyond itself to the divine but actually becomes the *incarnation* of the divine.

Wolterstorff describes two modes from everyday life in which the utterances or inscriptions of one person come to count as the speech acts of another: deputized speech and authorized speech.[5] Examples of deputized speech include the cases when an ambassador speaks

---

4. This Scripture and the next one are cited as given by Wolterstorff from the R. S. Pine-Coffin translation of *Confessions* (Baltimore: Penguin Books, 1961).

5. Wolterstorff, *Divine Discourse*, 38–51, 114–17, 186–87.

on behalf of a president or prime minister; when a capo in a crime family makes an offer, not to be refused, on behalf of the godfather; and when a parent sends one child to tell another that it's time to come in for dinner. The message is intended to be understood (had better be understood) as emanating from and carrying the authority of the deputizer, not the deputized messenger.

Authorized speech occurs when one speaker takes responsibility for what another, say a speechwriter or a ghostwriter, has already said. Or when back benchers in the British parliament chant, "Here, here!" Or when the boss signs a letter inscribed by the secretary.

In neither case is the degree of supervision crucial. The letter appropriated by the boss may have been dictated right down to the punctuation. But the boss may have been out of town when the need arose and the secretary, knowing the situation thoroughly, composed a letter of which the boss thought, upon returning and signing it, "I couldn't have said it better myself." By signing the letter in either case the boss gives executive authority to whatever threats or assurances or promises the letter contains. Similarly, whether the ambassador has received detailed and specific instructions about what to say or simply knows policy so well that this is not necessary, the message is (to be) understood as coming from the president or prime minister.

In just what sense the biblical writers may have been deputized before they wrote or authorized afterward is not easy to say. Perhaps it does not happen in each case once and for all, but Scripture is authorized whenever the inner testimony of the Holy Spirit bears witness to the divine origin and ownership of what is said. This is an important theological question that deserves closer attention than Wolterstorff is able to give it, but on the basis of what he does say, he puts forth a hermeneutics of what he calls "authorial discourse interpretation." To interpret the Bible properly is to ask the question: what speech acts did the author perform in writing this text?

In the case of biblical double discourse, there needs to be a double hermeneutic, asking the questions: What speech acts *did* the human writer perform in writing, say, the history of the kings of Israel or the epistle to Titus. What speech acts *does* God perform in addressing these writings to us now as the Word of God? Wolterstorff often uses the present tense when speaking of divine discourse. Paul's epistles may have been "a medium of divine discourse" at the time when Paul wrote them. But the Bible "may be [become?] a medium of *contemporary* divine discourse, a medium of God's *here and now* addressing you and me, the generating event being some such thing as our now being confronted with the text or *God's* now presenting the text to us."[6]

We might note in passing that these two questions are crucial to sermon preparation. The second one—What is God saying to us now in and through *this* text?—is an indispensable guard against preaching platitudes, that is, affirming important biblical truths that have no visible connection with the purported text(s) for the day. But to answer that question one must do the hard preparatory work of asking what the speaker or writer was saying to the original audience.

In placing major emphasis on the authority of the author in determining the meaning of the text, Wolterstorff takes sides on an issue that is central to the debate over objectivism versus relativism in interpretation. We shall come to this issue in due course and in so doing return to this issue of the tenses of divine discourse. But for the moment we need to notice the way authorial discourse interpretation is set off from "romantic" psychologism. Discourse occurs when someone says something about something to someone. We have three elements here: (1) the first someone is the *who* that speaks (perhaps by writing); (2) the something-about-something is the *what* that is said, which we might call the propositional content of the speech acts; and (3) the second someone is the *to whom* the speech acts are addressed.

Wolterstorff understandably places great emphasis on the *who* of divine discourse, but not for the reason Schleiermacher gives. The goal is not to refeel or reenact the inner psychic life of God, if it even makes sense to talk that way. Precisely because it is God who is speaking, the goal is to find out what commands and promises (law and gospel, if you like) God is making. In other words, Wolterstorff insists on the significance of the *who* precisely to direct our attention to the *what*. We are the *to whom*, and what we want to find out is the *what* that is addressed to us by a *who* that we take seriously. This applies to human authors as well. So Wolterstorff writes:

> The myth dies hard that to read a text for authorial discourse is to enter the dark world of the author's psyche. It is nothing of the

---

6. Ibid., 56; cf. 5, 7, 131. Wolterstorff adds that Antony and Augustine were addressed by God "*then and there*," that is, at the time when they heard or read.

sort. It is to read to discover what assertings, what promisings, what requestings, what commandings, are rightly to be ascribed to the author on the ground of her having set down the words she did in the situation in which she set them down. Whatever the dark demons and bright angels of the author's inner self that led her to take up this stance in public, it is that stance itself that we hope by reading to recover, not the dark demons and bright angels.[7]

Two things to notice here. First, while the phrase "intention of the author" is much bandied about in twentieth-century debates about objectivism in hermeneutics, it is inherently ambiguous. It might signify an event in the inner (hidden) life of the author, in which case to privilege the intention of the author would be to espouse "romantic" psychologism. Thus we might say, "She is a skillful diplomat (or poker player), so it's hard to know what her intentions are." But since normally what I intend to say is the same as what I actually say, that is, the speech acts I intend to perform are the ones I actually do perform, privileging the author's intention could be to espouse something like Wolterstorff's authorial discourse hermeneutics. The goal or target would not be the inner life ("dark demons and bright angels") of the author but the *what* of the discourse: what assertions, what promises, what commands are to be found here?

Of course, intention does not always correspond to performance. We all know about "Freudian" slips of the tongue. We know that what we say can hurt or offend someone although we did not intend such harm. And then there is Radames in Verdi's *Aida*. The Egyptian hero does not intend to tell the Ethiopian enemy a vital military secret. But by telling Aida what route they must take while eloping so as to avoid the Egyptian army, he tells her father Amonasro, the Ethiopian king in hiding, just what the latter needs to know. He did not intend to betray his country, but his speech act was just such a betrayal. For this reason Wolterstorff will give to the author alone the privilege of fixing the meaning of the text, though without speaking of the author's intentions. Some who do use this latter language will be closer to him than to Schleiermacher. We'll have to be careful if we are to avoid equivocation.

Second, the abandonment of psychologism does not in and of itself settle the question of objectivism. The quest for the speech

7. Ibid., 93.

acts performed by the author, whether human or divine, might be understood in relativistic terms for readers who are human and not divine. Wolterstorff himself leans strongly toward objectivism. Thus he says of authorial discourse interpretation, "The issue then is whether one's conclusions are correct, whether they are true— whether the discourser did in fact, by authoring or presenting this text, say what one claims he said."[8] Interpretation seems to be a fairly simple matter of getting it right or getting it wrong. Moreover, in a chapter titled "Has Scripture Become a Wax Nose?" Wolterstorff expresses the common anxiety that if one lets the camel of relativity get its nose in the tent it's all over and, as it is so often put, "anything goes." This vertigo of relativity, we can recall, is precisely what led Dilthey to his scientistic, rule-governed objectivism. Just for the record, except for a recent pizza ad, I can't find anyone who espouses an "anything goes" philosophy. Nietzsche, for example, whose perspectivism is a radical version of relativism, surely doesn't think Platonism or Christianity are just as good as his will-to-power naturalism. So I propose that we recognize the "anything goes" objection as the bugaboo it is and practice a fifty-year moratorium on the use of that phrase.

As we turn now to the issues that make up the debate over objectivism and relativism, we can do so with thanks to Wolterstorff for showing us why we should move away from "romantic" psychologism.

8. Ibid., 181.

4

Objectivism and Authorial Privilege

It seems that literary critics never tire of citing Oscar Wilde's claim that literary criticism "is the only civilized form of autobiography." In other words, literary criticism is "the record of one's own soul."[1] From theology there is George Tyrell's claim that the Christ of Adolf Harnack's famous *What Is Christianity?* "was only the reflection of a Liberal Protestant face [Harnack's own face], seen at the bottom of a deep well."[2] The suggestion in each case is that, for better (Wilde) or worse (Tyrell), interpretation is more about the interpreter than about the text, which becomes a mere pretext, like Wolterstorff's wax nose that can assume any shape.[3] The literary critic tells us about himself, and the theologian tells us about the tradition to which she belongs. The vertigo of relativity is the fear that this just may be the case. Since there are many

1. Oscar Wilde, "The Critic as Artist," in *The Portable Oscar Wilde*, ed. Richard Aldington and Stanley Weintraub, rev. ed. (New York: Penguin Books, 1981), 83. E.g., Geoffrey Hartman, "Passion and Literary Engagement," in *The Geoffrey Hartman Reader*, ed. Geoffrey H. Hartman and Daniel T. O'Hara (New York: Fordham University Press, 2004), 454.

2. George Tyrell, *Christianity at the Crossroads* (New York: Longmans, Green and Co., 1909), 44.

3. See chap. 3 above.

45

interpreters and traditions, there will be a "veritable plethora"[4] of interpretations, each relative to a different perspective. The text will be dissolved or dispersed at the cost of its identity. It will mean everything and therefore nothing. Thus Dilthey's question: "But where are the means to overcome the anarchy of opinions that then threatens to befall us?"[5]

Hirsch's Objectivism

Objectivism in hermeneutics is the belief (hope, claim, dogma) that while interpretation can become subjective in this manner, it need not. Done rightly, interpretation can free itself from particular perspectives and presuppositions, whether personal or communal, and give us *the* meaning of the text. Then we will have order instead of anarchy and knowledge instead of mere opinion. Dilthey will be able to sleep at night. We are familiar with the demand for this kind of objectivity in the legal sphere. Justices of the Supreme Court, we are told, should interpret the Constitution, not legislate or rewrite it. Regardless of personal views or changing circumstances, they can and should simply duplicate what the founding fathers said when they wrote the text.

In *Validity in Interpretation*,[6] E. D. Hirsch Jr. gives a passionate defense of hermeneutical objectivism. Unlike Dilthey, Hirsch has little to say about method as the rules for achieving universally valid interpretation (*VI* 12), that is, principles for weighing evidence (*VI* x). He does speak of "severe discipline" (*VI* ix) and "philological effort" (*VI* 57), echoing the linguistic side of Schleiermacher's method.[7] He also speaks of preunderstandings as hypotheses and in so doing assimilates interpretation to the

---

4. Longtime fans of Monday Night Football will recall that this is a phrase with which Howard Cosell used to torment "Dandy" Don Meredith.

5. See chap. 2 above for Dilthey's question and "the vertigo of relativity."

6. E. D. Hirsch Jr., *Validity in Interpretation* (New Haven, CT: Yale University Press, 1967). Subsequent references to this work in text and in the notes will be given with the abbreviation *VI*. For another version of objectivism contemporary with Hirsch's, see Emilio Betti, "Hermeneutics as the General Methodology of the *Geisteswissenschaften*," in *Contemporary Hermeneutics: Hermeneutics as Method, Philosophy, and Critique*, ed. Josef Bleicher (London: Routledge and Kegan Paul, 1980), 51–94.

7. See chap. 2 above.

hypothetico-deductive method of the natural sciences (*VI* 261, 264).[8]

But Hirsch's primary focus is on the *goal* of interpretation and the nature of the *object* that alone can satisfy that goal. The goal is "universally valid" or "absolutely valid" interpretation (*VI* 12, viii). This type of interpretation should give us "*the* meaning of the text" (*VI* 5). This does not mean absolute certainty. As in the natural sciences, here we are in a realm of fallibility and probability. We sometimes get it wrong, and even when we get it right we can't be absolutely certain that we have done so. The most that we can claim is that this or that is probably the best interpretation. But the goal is a consensus in which all interpreters arrive at an identical meaning (*VI* 256, 33).

What kind of object must the meaning of the text be in order to satisfy this requirement? It must be determinate, which means it must be "one, particular, self-identical, unchanging complex of meaning" (*VI* 47). This means that it is reproducible and re-cognizable. It is like the number seven. It is reproducible in that it is the very same, unchanged object when I think it in the morning, when I think it in the afternoon, and when you think it in the evening. It is re-cognizable in that when I come back to it in the afternoon and you come to it in the evening it is the same as it was in the morning and can, at least in principle, be understood by me in the afternoon and by you in the evening in exactly the same way as I understood it in the morning. There may be many occasions of understanding (acts of consciousness) but only one substance or content of understanding (object of consciousness), namely, *the* meaning of the text. Thus the desert fathers, the Geneva Calvinists, the American slaves, and today's Amish can and should understand the Bible to say exactly the same thing. One implication of this view is that while my or "our" current understanding of the Bible can claim to be *the* meaning of the text, the rest of Christian history is a series of unfortunate misinterpretations. Anxiety about relativism morphs into arrogance.

Like Wolterstorff, Hirsch appeals to the prerogative of the author to provide such a meaning. The text means what the author meant (*VI* 1, 8). The author is *the* determiner of textual meaning (*VI* 246, 248).

---

8. The phrase "hypothetico-deductive" refers to the once popular understanding of science and (1) the formulation of hypotheses, (2) the deduction of what would follow by way of experience if the hypotheses were true, and (3) the performing of experiments to see whether the predicted consequences actually occur.

The task of interpretation is to reproduce what the author meant. Hirsch sometimes speaks of the author's intention (*VI* 17–18), but like Wolterstorff he disavows romantic psychologism. To speak of authorial intention is not to speak of the author's inner life, private experiences, or mental processes, much less the author's personality. Authorial intention is about the public, shareable meanings the author offers to us. They are like the number seven, not like my hidden intention to rob the bank.

Perhaps to avoid the ambiguity of talk about intention, Hirsch prefers much of the time to link meaning to consciousness, which he also interprets in terms of will. The text means what the author wills to convey (*VI* 31, 46–49). Words by themselves, as audible sounds or visible designs, don't mean anything. They require the human consciousness as will to be involved when someone says something about something to someone. Meaning is the something-about-something in this formula, and to keep it single and unchanging—a proper object of objective knowledge—Hirsch ties it to the first someone, the author, rather than the second someone, the hearer or reader, of whom there are many. Although he does not use the language of speech-act theory, Hirsch's strategy is very similar to that of Wolterstorff's authorial discourse interpretation in privileging the author as *the* source of meaning.

Like Dilthey, who worries about an anarchy of mere opinion, and Wolterstorff, who worries that Scripture may become a wax nose in any different-strokes-for-different-folks hermeneutics, Hirsch has been smitten with the vertigo of relativity. For this reason he wages battle against any suggestion of textual autonomy, which is the notion that textual meaning has any independence from authorial intention, consciousness, or will and that authorial consciousness is not the unilateral determiner of textual meaning. He describes the danger in a variety of ways.

- He worries about the view that "the author brings the words and the reader the meaning" (*VI* 1).
- He worries that textual autonomy means that the text "leads an afterlife of its own, totally cut off from the life of its author" (*VI* 1).
- He worries about "authorial irrelevance . . . once the author has been ruthlessly banished as *the* determiner of the text's meaning" (*VI* 3; emphasis added; cf. 11–12).

- He worries that the critic, that is, the reader, will replace the author with the result that "one interpretation is as valid as another" (*VI* 4; cf. 11).
- He worries that there will be a multiplicity of meanings, "each carrying as much authority as the next" (*VI* 5).
- He worries that if the reader is allowed to get a nose in the tent, "textual meaning could change in any respect [and] there could be no principle for distinguishing a valid interpretation from a false one" (*VI* 6).
- He worries that "IT DOES NOT MATTER WHAT AN AUTHOR MEANS—ONLY WHAT HIS TEXT SAYS," in which case "any reading of a text would be 'valid,' since any reading would correspond to what the text 'says'—to that reader." No author would have the right to complain about being misinterpreted (*VI* 10). The slogan for these last four worries might be "Anything goes when you've got a wax nose."
- He worries that readers will feel authorized to proceed "unencumbered by a concern for the author's original intention" (*VI* 246).
- He worries that we will take the text to be so indeterminate that it "means whatever we take it to mean" (*VI* 249).
- He worries about the legal version of textual autonomy according to which "a law means what the judges take it to mean" (*VI* 250).
- He concludes that under the regime of textual autonomy "there is little point in writing books," especially about hermeneutical matters (*VI* 251).

The reader will have noticed that most of these worries are front-loaded at the outset of Hirsch's book (the others coming in his critique of Gadamer). The rhetorical effect is not unlike that of a presidential speech that begins, "Terrorism! Terrorism! Terrorism! Al-Qaeda! Al-Qaeda! Al-Qaeda!" with the not too subtle implication that anyone who disagrees with whatever follows is soft on terrorism and sympathetic to al-Qaeda. So we should be on our guard. But just as terrorism is a real threat, so various forms of relativism raise genuine and troubling questions. We need to examine carefully what follows the opening salvo, without allowing our critical faculties to be overwhelmed by a rhetorical strategy of "shock and awe." What we must keep in mind is that to say that certain ideas, beliefs, practices, or interpretations are relative to this cultural or historical horizon is to say that they are conditioned by that context and would be different, or even impossible, in other contexts. Thus the biblical interpretations of the desert fathers are relative to their mode of monastic life. Since only God is absolute and we are relative, this kind of relativity shows up all over the place. But it is not at all the same as the relativism that says "Anything goes," every interpretation is as good as every other one. To equate the two is to succumb to sloppy thinking.

Questions for Hirsch

I believe that the best response to the objectivist tradition in hermeneutics is to take a close look at some relativistic versions of philosophical hermeneutics, none of which implies that "anything goes." If the reader will be patient (and even if not) we will get to that in our next chapter. But already there are at least four questions that arise directly out of Hirsch's presentation.

Question One: Who Are the Bad Guys?

It isn't always clear that Hirsch isn't tilting at windmills or setting straw men afire. He often doesn't identify anyone who holds a particular version of the view that so worries him. But sometimes he does. The first of his worries above not only is attributed to Northrop Frye but also comes from his own words in a quotation with which Hirsch opens his own jeremiad: "It has been said of Boehme that his books are like a picnic to which the author brings the words and the reader the meaning. The remark may have been intended as a sneer at Boehme, but it is an exact description of all works of literary art without exception" (*VI* 1). This is explicitly not a general hermeneutics for culturally significant texts; nor is it clear that Frye is wrong, much less dangerously wrong. In reading novels, and especially poetry, are not the moods and images evoked, which differ from reader to reader, so essential to the meaning of the text that to speak of the text's meaning in abstraction from them is to misunderstand it, along with the genre to which it belongs, from the start? When texts rely heavily on metaphors and other figures of speech, does it make sense to ask for *the* meaning of the text? Do we really want to assimilate the meaning of *Moby-Dick* or "Stopping by Woods on a Snowy Evening" to the meaning of "e=mc^2" or "the cat is on the mat"? Wouldn't that be a case of "I had to kill the patients (texts) in order to save them (from multiple interpretations)"?

Similarly we would need to examine closely the texts of Eliot, Pound, Heidegger, and Jung to see whether, as Hirsch suggests, they actually affirm an autonomy of the text such that "it leads an afterlife of its own, totally cut off from the life of its author" (*VI* 1–2) and, if so, just what these texts mean. Only someone who failed Logic 101 can think that to deny that the author is the sole source of meaning in a text is to present the text as "totally cut off from" the author.

When the New Critics, a major target of Hirsch (and Wolterstorff), say this sort of thing, what they seem to mean is something like this:

> We often don't know who the author of a text is, and, as in the case of "Homer" or the Epistle to the Hebrews, all we know in general about him (or her) we learn from the text we seek to understand. So we have to interpret it without drawing on any external information about the life of the author. Even when we have independent biographical knowledge, it is best to bracket it and restrict our search for the meaning(s) of the text to the text itself. This calls for the "severe discipline" of close reading and is in no way the suggestion that any reading is just as good as any other.

This may involve a self-denying ordinance that is not the only fruitful way to read literary texts, but anyone who has been taught to read poetry under the influence of New Criticism knows that it is not an invitation to anarchy. Interpretations must be supported by evidence from the text. Nor are we dealing with "authorial irrelevance." A classic repudiation of psychologism and a canonical text of New Criticism is "The Intentional Fallacy" by W. K. Wimsatt and Monroe Beardsley.[9] Hirsch acknowledges that Wimsatt and

9. W. K. Wimsatt and Monroe Beardsley, "The Intentional Fallacy," *Sewanee Review* 54 (1946). Reprinted in William K. Wimsatt Jr., *The Verbal Icon: Studies in the Meaning of Poetry* (Lexington: University of Kentucky Press, 1954), and frequently anthologized.

Beardsley "carefully distinguished between three types of intentional evidence, acknowledging that two of them are proper and admissible," but he bemoans the fact that "their careful distinction and qualifications have now vanished in the popular version which consists in the false and facile dogma that what an author intended is irrelevant to the meaning of his text" (*VI* 11–12). But he provides no example in support of this lament.

Question Two: What about Unconscious Meanings?

Hirsch tells us that texts don't express all that their authors have in mind, and they say more than their authors are aware of. In this sense there are unconscious meanings, and yet he insists on linking meaning to intention in the sense of conscious will. How so?

We need to realize that he is not talking about the unconscious in the Freudian sense of repression. Whatever issues might arise for hermeneutics are not part of this discussion.[10] By "unconscious" he means simply "not actually thinking about," as in "While I was trying to solve this equation, I wasn't thinking about how many roses were used in last year's Rose Bowl Parade." Of course, those roses are not likely to be part of the unconscious meaning of my discourse about the equation. What Hirsch has in mind is something like this: When I say "I like dogs," I may be thinking about Tippy, beloved pet of my childhood, and Merlin, our son's dog who thinks he owns the whole house. I'm not thinking about the shih tzu Aunt Susie used to have or the Weimaraner she will get next year. But they belong to the meaning of my statement, "I like dogs." If it turns out that I can't stand shih tzus and am afraid of Weimaraners, my statement will have proven false or at least misleading. This is because *dogs* signifies a consciously willed *type* (we might say a universal concept) that includes more instances than I (can) have in mind at any given moment (*VI* 17–18, 48–52).

Hirsch says three things about such types: (1) they have boundaries (or else meaning could not be a determinate object of thought); (2) they have multiple instances; and (3) the meaning they express "can never be limited to a unique, concrete content" (*VI* 49–50). This seems to mean that these types are somewhat determinate and somewhat indeterminate; if this is so, Hirsch may have let a camel

10. For Hirsch's discussion of Freud, see *VI* 122–26.

get an unwelcome nose in his hermeneutical tent. Is Pluto a planet? Why is the boundary between plants and animals not all that clear for biologists? Perhaps my discourse about planets and plants is not as fully determinate as Hirsch would like. Nor, perhaps, is the text of the Constitution or the Bible.

Question Three: Why the Banishment and Irrelevance of the Reader?

Hirsch tells us that words as mere physical objects or events, sounds or marks, are not meaningful. "A word sequence means nothing in particular until somebody either means something by it or understands something from it. There is no magic land of meanings outside human consciousness" (*VI* 4). The someone who means is, of course, the author, while the someone who understands is the reader (interpreter). In the language of discourse theory, they are the first and second someones in the formula "someone says something about something to someone."

Given this location of meaning within the human consciousness, Hirsch adds a second point. "The meanings that are actualized by the reader are either shared with the author or belong to the reader alone" (*VI* 23). The former is what Hirsch requires; the latter is what he fears. We know that what he means by a meaning *shared* by reader and author is a meaning unilaterally determined by the author and universally duplicated by the reader, that is, reproduced in an unmodified identity by all readers. We also know that for Hirsch when meaning belongs to the reader *alone* we have the anarchy of opinion feared by Dilthey, for there are many readers, particular as individuals or as communities and traditions of interpretation, and there will always be a "veritable plethora" of interpretations, each allegedly as good as any other.

Here we encounter the radical either/or that shapes Hirsch's hermeneutics from start to finish. Either the author alone determines meaning or the reader alone determines meaning. In the first case, objectivity and universal validity are possible in principle; in the second case we have an "anything goes" relativism in which there is no terra firma. The vertigo of relativity is a response to the vortex of radical perspectivism, a plurality and particularity without principle.

But are these the only two options? Might not the meaning(s) of a text be coproduced by author and reader, the product of their interaction? Might not each contribute to the determinacy of meaning without requiring that it be absolutely determinate? If the author has a legitimate role, without needing to be an autocrat, then the text cannot mean just anything that any reader takes it to mean. There will be boundaries, as Hirsch requires. But if the reader also plays a role, these boundaries will be sufficiently generous to allow that a given text might legitimately mean somewhat different things to different people in different circumstances. Moreover, this way of viewing understanding would help us to make sense of the obvious fact that differences of interpretation are the rule rather than the exception in literature, law, and theology.

Over against this possibility, if we ask why Hirsch insists on his rigid either/or, his my-way-or-the-highway hermeneutics (author as absolute monarch of meaning versus reader as textual terrorist), the answer is quite clear. Only in this way can he defend his brand of objectivism with its universal, indeed absolute, validity in interpretation. One is reminded of the little boy whose father overheard him telling a whopper. "My little puppy was being chased by a big, angry dog who came just this close to catching him. He would have caught him, too, but my little puppy climbed up a tree and sat safely on the branch, just as the little bird escaped from the big, bad cat in *Peter and the Wolf*." "Son," the father said sternly, "you mustn't tell stories like that. You know that puppies can't climb trees!" To which the lad replied, "But Daddy, he just got to." This sometimes happens in philosophy. Someone decides that we just "got to" have some kind of knowledge, and presto! Suddenly we have a theory assuring us that we do, or at least can, have it.

But do we really got to? Is it self-evident that Hirsch's ideal is possible or even desirable? Is it, perhaps, dangerous?[11] Is it not itself the product of a particular tradition, one that includes Plato

11. Paul Ricoeur thinks so. In an interview he says, "A common or identical history cannot be reached—and should not be attempted—because it is part of life that there are conflicts [including conflicts of interpretation]. The challenge is to bring conflicts to the level of discourse and not let them degenerate into violence, to accept that they tell history in their own words as we tell our history in our own words. . . . Sometimes consensus is a dangerous game" (*Debates in Continental Philosophy: Conversations with Contemporary Thinkers*, ed. Richard Kearney [New York: Fordham University Press, 2004], 46–47; cf. 108–9).

and Descartes, whose ideal of knowledge is largely determined by mathematics? Should those of us interested in interpreting the Bible assimilate its texts to a series of equations? Doesn't the Bible point us in a different direction by telling us that we need four different interpretations of the life, death, and resurrection of Jesus as well as epistles interpreting the Christ event by a variety of authors? Should we be surprised or dismayed when each of these Gospels is subject to a variety of interpretations? Must we assume that our interpretation is the only right one and that all the believers throughout Christian history who depart from our party line are simply wrong?

Question Four: What Are the Implications of Shared Conventions?

We have seen Hirsch tie verbal meaning to authorial intention as consciously willed type. But there are two further, important claims: (1) "The willed type must be a shared type in order for communication to occur"; (2) this means:

> the willed type has to fall within known conventions in order to be shared. . . . Our chances of making a correct preliminary guess about the nature of someone's verbal meaning are enormously increased by the limitations imposed on that meaning through cultural norms and conventions. A single linguistic sign can represent an identical meaning for two persons because its possible meanings have been limited by convention." (*VI* 66–67, 262)

For the moment let us overlook that Hirsch assumes what is very much in question, namely, that when two persons successfully communicate they share "an identical meaning." What is of interest is the link between shared meaning and cultural conventions, which include linguistic conventions but far exceed them. If identical meaning is to emerge and if meaning is tied to cultural conventions, it would seem that the cultural conventions at work in my understanding must be identical with those at work in yours. But this is dubious even among contemporaries within the same country. Successful socialization makes it possible for people to live together in spite of cultural conventions that differ from middle-class white males to upper-class white females to middle-class minorities to poor rural whites to poor urban minorities and so forth. We could also ascribe the changes to religious differences as well as those of class, gender, and race. Then there is the perennial and perennially moving genera- tion gap. When we move from where we are to different continents and different eras, it becomes even clearer how much difference there is among the cultural conventions that govern how we mean and how we understand. At this point the argument risks lapsing into the supposedly disavowed psychologism that says we can un- derstand others only by entering into their inner psychic lives and seeing the world or the text not through our own eyes but through eyes shaped by cultural conventions dramatically different from our own. Here again it appears that Hirsch's own theory of meaning opens the door to something rather different from the objectivity and universality he wants to affirm.

It is said in sports that you can't beat anybody with nobody and in politics that you can't just be "against them," you have to be for something. If you don't like the current policy, you must suggest an alternative. I've suggested some problems with Hirsch's theory, but the acid test is whether I can present a viable alternative. It is to that task I now turn.

5

Revoking Authorial Privilege

The Death of the Author

Almost simultaneously with Hirsch's plea to absolutize the author, three French postmodernist authors sought to revoke the author's privilege of being the sole determiner of a fully determinate text. In 1968 Roland Barthes published "The Death of the Author."[1] In 1969 Michel Foucault added "What Is an Author?"[2] Then in several texts from the late 1960s, Jacques Derrida joined in to make it a trio.[3]

In the spirit of Mark Twain, we might say that reports of the author's death have been exaggerated, both by the rhetoric of our French trio and by the careless reading of their texts. They do not suggest, as one might suppose in the spirit of Hirsch, that the author is totally irrelevant to the meaning of the text but rather that the author is not the sole producer of its meaning. One would

1. Roland Barthes, "The Death of the Author," in *Image—Music—Text*, trans. Stephen Heath (New York: Noonday, 1977), 142–48. See note 3 of this chapter.

2. Michel Foucault, "What Is an Author?" in *The Foucault Reader*, ed. Paul Rabinow (New York: Pantheon, 1984), 101–20. See note 3 of this chapter.

3. For a discussion of all three, including the Derrida references, see Merold Westphal, "Kierkegaard and the Anxiety of Authorship," in *The Death and Resurrection of the Author?* ed. William Irwin (Westport, CT: Greenwood, 2002), 23–43. The essays by Barthes and Foucault are included in this volume and will be cited from it.

have a hard time getting out of Logic 101 if one insisted on treating "X is not solely responsible for Y" as logically equivalent to "X is not in any way responsible for Y." That Germany, for example, was not solely responsible for World War I is not the same as, nor does it entail that, Germany was not in any way responsible for World War I. Accordingly, to deny that the author is *the unilateral source* of a text's meaning is not to deny that the author plays an important role.

It is the weaker claim about the limits of authorial prerogative that is maintained in the French texts, and our trio unites in using theological language to make their point. According to familiar versions of theism, God is Creator, and the world has all and only those features that God (intended to) put there; if there is a certain indeterminacy due to creaturely freedom, that is only because God (intended to) put creaturely freedom in the world. Similarly, according to the view our trio wishes to dispute, the author is Creator of the text; it has all and only those meanings that the author (intended to) put there. In other words, it is a very particular kind of human author whose death is being announced, namely, one who never existed in the first place. Real authors do not create meaning in the way God created the world. They are neither the Alpha (pure, unconditioned origin) of meaning nor the Omega (ultimate goal) of interpretation. For this reason interpretation cannot be understood as deciphering, for in deciphering the meaning is already there, fixed and final (author as Alpha), though disguised by code, and the task is to discover and reproduce the author's meaning (author as Omega).[4]

Of course, as atheists these authors do not believe in God as Creator of the world. At times it can seem as if they are saying, in a Nietzschean tone of voice, "We as knowers and more particularly as authors are not absolute; we do not divinely dispose over truth and meaning. So there is no God, and all truth and meaning is relative." Of course, this is a non sequitur and would not help you get a good grade in Logic 101. From the fact that we are not God it doesn't follow that no one else is. But the believing soul who is

4. The idea that meaning is fixed in inner experience prior to its encoding in language for the sake of outer communication is the expressivist view of language discussed in relation to "romantic" psychologism. See chap. 2 above. Our trio agrees in rejecting it and viewing language as internal rather than external to experience.

content to point this out has missed the important point. Atheistic postmodernism sometimes seems to say (fallaciously):

I am not God; therefore there is no God.[5]

The believer says:

Someone else is God; therefore I am not God.

The important point here is the deep agreement between the two parties that we are not God, that we are relative (conditioned by factors that are neither universal nor unchanging) and not absolute, however different the accompanying beliefs about God's own reality may be. The finitude of human discourse that various philosophies, even atheistic ones, assert on more or less phenomenological grounds just might be very much like the finitude the believer wants to assert on theological grounds.

For our French trio, the finitude of the author in relation to the text is expressed in a double relativity. In the first place, human authors "create" meaning only relative to the language available to them, the language in which they live and move and have their being. They are at most cocreators of meaning, for they did not create this language (though the great ones modify it); rather, this language shapes and conditions their thought in ways of which they are unaware and over which they do not preside. Barthes expresses this with typical rhetorical hyperbole, insisting that "it is language that speaks, not the author."[6] Taken in isolation, an all too prevalent practice of those afraid to acknowledge the relativity of their own thought, this could be taken as the announcement of utter "authorial irrelevance" (Hirsch). But if one reads the statement in context, a practice highly to be commended, the author banished is only the (fictitious) author who is the owner of language, the author who in godlike sovereignty is the creator of language but is not conditioned by the language(s) that have always preceded, made possible, and limited the work of the author.

---

5. Or perhaps, "The only cognitive activities I am familiar with are finite and relative, so all such activities are finite and relative." Of course, there is no contradiction in holding to both the "only" and the "all" clause as long as one does not suggest that the latter follows from the former.

6. Barthes, "Death of the Author," 4. In other words, "the writer can only imitate a gesture that is always anterior, never original" (ibid., 6).

The relativity of authorial meaning to the language that always precedes and pre-forms both the act of writing and indeed the author's very being need not be taken too narrowly. By the author's language we can understand not only the grammar, syntax, and vocabulary in and through which the author comes into being but also the texts and cultural practices that are the author's womb and family. Even in this broader sense, the relativity of meaning need not by itself lead to an "anything goes" hermeneutics. The notion of interpretation as deciphering a preexistent (to the interpreter) meaning can be maintained, as it is in Hirsch. He acknowledges the importance of "conventions."[7] But only if, expanding Schleiermacher's linguistic and psychological modes of research to include the historical and cultural dimensions of authorial formation, one might still hope and even claim to decipher the text's fixed and prior (to the interpreter) meaning by studying the contextual factors that condition its production. What now counts as *the* meaning of the text is the meaning the author (intended to) put into it, granted that the author does not create meaning ex nihilo but under conditions that we can discover and take into account. When theologians speak of grammatical-historical interpretation of the Bible, they are referring to just such discovery and taking into account.

It is the second relativity of authorial meaning presented by "death of the author" French thought that threatens the objectivism of thinkers like Hirsch and Dilthey (and many theologians, academic, pastoral, and lay). It is the relativity of authorial meaning to the reader. Barthes ends his essay by telling us that "the birth of the reader must be at the cost of the death of the author."[8] By now we should have learned not to assume that this means the supposedly godlike author is to be replaced by an equally godlike reader who creates meaning ex nihilo, "unencumbered by a concern for the author's original intention," so that "one interpretation is as valid as another."[9] We have every reason to expect that the finitude of the author will be mirrored in the finitude of the reader, who will be no pure origin of meaning but will be conditioned by prior meanings, including those that stem from the author as well as those that stem from the reader's own grammatical-historical location.

7. See chap. 4, above.
8. Barthes, "Death of the Author," 7.
9. The quotations are from Hirsch. See chap. 4 above.

Here author and reader are cocreators of textual meaning. This is a genuine threat to hermeneutical objectivism, for there are many readers (including the same reader at different times and in different circumstances) and many traditions of reading, so the notion of *the* meaning of the text becomes highly problematic. When the text is understood as giving rise to meaning at the site of conversation between author and reader, there will be different meanings because there will be different conversations.

In affirming with Barthes the importance of the reader, Michel Foucault and Jacques Derrida introduce themes that will require our close attention as we proceed further. Foucault suggests, in a mixture of hyperbole and antipsychologism, that "the author function will disappear" as our society changes and that instead of asking "Who really spoke? . . . And what part of his deepest self did he express in his discourse?" we will address questions such as "Who can appropriate it for himself? . . . What difference does it make who is speaking?"[10] Of course this will not work for a love letter addressed to us or for the Bible if we think of it as God's love letter addressed to us. But the question of who wrote "Homer" or "Shakespeare" or the Epistle to the Hebrews (humanly speaking) might well seem far less important than the question of possible appropriation. What might we learn from this text, and how might it change our lives?

Derrida suggests that when we give up the idea that texts have an absolute origin in which meaning is fully present prior to its inscription and the corresponding idea that interpretation is deciphering, we will be able to give ourselves "to an active interpretation."[11] The *active* role of the reader that goes beyond a deciphering that aims merely to reproduce a meaning already complete in itself will require, along with the notion of *appropriation*, careful scrutiny as we proceed.

Having let the reader get a camel-like nose in the tent, let us now ask if we are on a slippery slope to a relativism where "anything goes" and where the text becomes a wax nose that can mean anything to anyone. Undoubtedly so, if that is the only alternative to allowing the author to be Absolute Monarch of Meaning or Divine Dispenser

10. Foucault, "What Is an Author?" 22.

11. Jacques Derrida, "Structure, Sign, and Play in the Discourse of the Human Sciences," in *Writing and Difference*, trans. Alan Bass (Chicago: University of Chicago Press, 1978), 292.

of Determinacy. But we have already learned in Logic 101 not to infer authorial irrelevance from the denial of authorial sovereignty. Or, to use a political analogy, the president of the United States does not rule by divine right with unconditioned authority. He is under constraints by Congress and the courts. But only a muddle-headed monarchist would complain that as president he has been banished to utter irrelevance and plays no significant role in the enactment and enforcement of laws in the United States.

Hermeneutically this means that the death of the absolute author is not the absolute death of the author. Authorial meaning is still important. Although interpretation is not deciphering as the mere reproduction of a prior, fixed, encoded meaning, there will be a reproductive aspect to interpretation. While denying that it is the whole story, Derrida emphasizes the importance and limited role of this aspect.

> This moment of doubling commentary [the reproductive aspect] should no doubt have its place in a critical reading. To recognize and respect all its classical exigencies is not easy and requires all the instruments of traditional criticism [e.g., grammatical-historical exegesis]. Without this recognition and this respect, critical production [active interpretation] would risk developing in any direction and authorize itself to say almost anything. [Note that Derrida is no fan of "anything goes."] But this indispensable guardrail has always only *protected*, it has never *opened* a reading.[12]

Gadamer puts the same point more briefly. "Not just occasionally but always, the meaning of a text goes beyond its author. That is why understanding is not merely a reproductive but always a productive activity as well."[13] In his eagerness to make Gadamer look dangerous,

12. Jacques Derrida, *Of Grammatology*, trans. Gayatri Chakravorty Spivak (Baltimore: Johns Hopkins University Press, 1976), 158. The "guardrail" need not be a sufficient guide to interpretation in order to be a necessary one, for "the enterprise of interpretation becomes arbitrary when the text can provide no check on its own interpretation" (Michael Root, "The Joint Declaration on the Doctrine of Justification," in *Rereading Paul Together: Protestant and Catholic Perspectives on Justification*, ed. David E. Aune [Grand Rapids: Baker Academic, 2006], 72).

13. Hans-Georg Gadamer, *Truth and Method*, trans. Joel Weinsheimer and Donald G. Marshall, 2nd ed. (New York: Crossroad, 1989), 296 (same page in the 2004 ed.). The German text reads, "Daher ist Verstehen kein nur reproductives, sondern stets auch ein productives Verhalten." See the fuller citation of this passage in chap. 7. Ricoeur emphasizes the productive dimension when he writes, "The problem for a hermeneutics

Hirsch misquotes this passage, leaving out the "merely" and the "as well" so that the (mis)quotation becomes, "Understanding is not a reproductive but always a productive activity." He takes this to be a denial "that the text has *any* determinate meaning." But it seems that it is Hirsch who has, by his practice, banned the author to irrelevance so that the text "means whatever we take it to mean."[14]

The Autonomy of the Text

Central to the hermeneutical theory of Paul Ricoeur is the thesis of the autonomy of the text. Less rhetorically flamboyant than talk of the "death of the author," this claim is a revocation of authorial privilege virtually identical with that of his three French compatriots. It is a "threefold autonomy: with respect to the intention of the author; with respect to the cultural situation and all the sociological conditions of the production of the text; and finally, with respect to the original addressee."[15]

This autonomy is not a total independence. It does not banish the author, and by implication the original context and original audience, to irrelevance. Ricoeur is quite explicit about this:

> Not that we can conceive of a text without an author; the tie between the speaker and the discourse is not abolished, but distended and complicated. . . . The text's career escapes the finite horizon lived by its author. What the text says now matters more than what the author meant to say, and every exegesis unfolds its procedures within the circumference of a meaning that has broken its moorings to the psychology of its author. (*HHS* 201)

Indeed, "the 'world' of the *text* may explode the world of the *author*." We are obviously dealing with another repudiation of

---

of language is not to rediscover some pristine immediacy [the mind of the author hidden behind the text] but to mediate again and again in a new and more creative fashion" (Paul Ricoeur, *Debates in Continental Philosophy: Conversations with Contemporary Thinkers*, ed. Richard Kearney [New York: Fordham University Press, 2004], 106).

14. E. D. Hirsch, *Validity in Interpretation* (New Haven, CT: Yale University Press, 1967), 249.

15. Paul Ricoeur, *Hermeneutics and the Human Sciences: Essays on Language, Action, and Interpretation*, ed. and trans. John B. Thompson (New York: Cambridge University Press, 1981), 91; hereafter *HHS*.

"romantic" psychologism and expressivism. Like Wolterstorff (see chap. 3), Ricoeur understands writing to be the objectification of discourse in which "someone says something to someone about something. Hermeneutics, I shall say, remains the art of discerning the discourse in the work" (*HHS* 138). The someone who speaks does not disappear, but attention is focused on the "something about something." This is because in reading "what we want to understand is not *something hidden behind the text* [the author's inner life or Wolterstorff's "dark demons and bright angels"] but *something disclosed in front of it*, namely '*what the text is about*'" (*HHS* 218; emphasis added). What is "in front of" the text rather than hidden behind it is a world, a complex of meaning and truth that is "opened" by the text (*HHS*, 53, 93, 111, 139) and thereby "proposed" as a mode of being-in-the-world that we might "inhabit" (*HHS* 112, 142).

This is not how Wolterstorff would put it, but it is not so different either. With special reference to the biblical text, Ricoeur wants to know what promises, commands, and so forth are to be found. He is looking for the discourse in the work. Taken together we might say that the promises and commands constitute a world in which we might live, a world of biblical faith. "Fair enough," Wolterstorff might reply, "but why shouldn't the author's speech act in its original context be what determines what promises, commands, and so forth the text contains, together constituting the 'world in front of the text'"? We have already seen that in his notion of a double discourse Wolterstorff himself opens the door to restricting the human author's privilege. The double hermeneutics that takes the biblical mode of double discourse into account first asks, "What *did* the human author say to the original audience?" and then "What *is* God saying to us here and now through those human speech acts inscribed in Scripture?" The assumption is that the two questions do not necessarily have the same answer, for otherwise there would be no need for a double hermeneutics.[16] Surely, to use his example of double discourse, the child whom Augustine heard singing "*tolle lege*" was not commanding any adult to read the

16. Thus, e.g., Ched Myers writes that though his reading of Mark "tries to maintain a synoptic view of what the Gospel *meant* in its own socio-historical context and what it *means* in ours, these two necessary tasks of interpretation are not identical, nor can they be carried out simultaneously" (Myers, *Binding the Strong Man: A Political Reading of Mark's Story of Jesus* [Maryknoll, NY: Orbis Books, 1988], xxvii).

Epistle to the Romans. But to Augustine as a hearer in a different context from the child's possible playmates, that was what God was telling him to do.

As with the death-of-the-author trio, it is the role of the reader that limits the sovereignty of the author for Ricoeur. The appropriation, response, and even compliance of the reader helps to produce and determine the meaning (*HHS* 112–13, 158, 161); and since there are different readers in different contexts, there will be different meanings, not *the* meaning of the text. Ricoeur speaks of "an unlimited series of readings" in view of the many different contexts in which many different readers interpret the text, no one of which is final (*HHS* 139). Remember our friends the desert fathers, the Geneva Calvinists, the American slaves, and today's Amish.

Through writing, "discourse escapes the limits of being face to face. It no longer has a visible auditor. An unknown, invisible reader has become the unprivileged addressee of the discourse" (*HHS* 203). It is this invisibility that gives the text an autonomy, an independence from authorial intention. The author is not a godlike, infinite creator of meaning. To call each of these readers or reading communities and traditions, who are invisible to the author and the original audience, "unprivileged" is simply to say that the absolute author is not replaced by an absolute reader but by one whose authority is as limited, relative to a particular context, as that of the author.

If we ask why meaning "escapes" the immediate context of the author and the original audience, Ricoeur gives us two reasons beyond the obvious empirical fact that legal, literary, and religious texts are regularly interpreted differently by different interpreters in different circumstances. One is the polysemy of language, even ordinary language. By polysemy, Ricoeur means simply that meaning is contextual, that words have different meanings in different contexts. The meaning of a text cannot be determined by a passive, merely mirroring *intuition* but only by an active *interpretation* (*HHS* 44, 106–8). The role of the author's context is not "abolished" but "complicated" (see above) by the role of the reader's context, which inevitably becomes part of the hermeneutical circle in which interpretation occurs. While this is true of ordinary discourse, it is especially true of metaphorical language (*HHS* 211).[17]

---

17. See Paul Ricoeur, *The Rule of Metaphor: Multi-disciplinary Studies of the Creation of Meaning in Language*, trans. Robert Czerny (London: Routledge and Kegan Paul, 1978).

The second reason is at least as important as the first. It reflects
the holism we have already encountered in Schleiermacher. Meaning
is contextual in the sense that the meaning of parts of a text is dependent on the meaning of the whole, and the meaning of a whole text
is dependent on various larger wholes—linguistic and cultural—to
which it belongs. Interpretation is construal rather than intuition for
the simple reason that no one, neither the author nor the reader, is
in actual possession of the whole that would give fully final and determinate meaning (HHS 109, 211). Ricoeur writes, "Now the ideal
of an intuitive foundation is the ideal of an interpretation which,
at a certain point, would pass into full vision. This is what Gadamer calls the hypothesis of 'total mediation'" (HHS 109; cf. 211).
Like our French trio, both Gadamer and Ricoeur see the historical
finitude of both author and reader as precluding this "pretension"
to "absolute knowledge" (HHS 109). Biblical faith has theological
reasons for agreeing. We are creatures, not the Creator.

In any case, the result of such a full vision of the totality of meaning and truth implicit in a text might itself be a complex plurality
of different meanings. We are reminded of the six blind men from
Hindustan, each of whom had a grasp of part of what an elephant
is but none of whom could grasp the complex totality that is an
elephant. The meaning of the elephant is the coherent harmony
of all their perspectives, not the elimination of all their different
standpoints in favor of the view from nowhere.

Consider an example from Wolterstorff that shows how a single
utterance can rightly have different meanings for different hearers. At
dinner Mom says, "Only two more days till Christmas." To her young
children, who think that Christmas will never come, her speech act
is a word of comfort and hope. But to her husband "she may have
said, in a rather arch and allusive way, that he must stop delaying and
get his shopping done. One locutionary act [vocal utterance], several
illocutionary acts [words of comfort and hope, words of warning,
even command], different ones for different addressees."[18]

As Wolterstorff tells the story, Mom is the godlike author whose
words have just the meanings she puts into them. They mean different
things to different hearers so that the meaning of her discourse is
a plurality of different meanings. In godlike sovereignty she knows

---

18. Nicholas Wolterstorff, Divine Discourse: Philosophical Reflections on the Claim
That God Speaks (New York: Cambridge University Press, 1995), 55.

all the hearers and controls the meaning each receives. But suppose they weren't all at dinner and Mom didn't know that Dad was in a position to overhear her. Dad would rightly take Mom's speech act to be one of reminder, warning, and perhaps even command, though that was not the meaning she (intended to) put into her discourse. The situation would be like that of Radames (see chap. 3), who didn't know that Aida's father, Amonasro, was listening and that he therefore had at least one audience of which he was not aware. The meaning of Radames's utterance escaped the horizon of its author and its original, intended audience (Aida) precisely because of the invisibility of at least one additional audience. This is the situation of human authors in general, biblical or otherwise.

Does this mean that anything goes, that a text can mean whatever any audience takes it to mean? Hardly! Ricoeur has already insisted that the role of the author is not "abolished" but only "complicated" by the plurality of invisible readers. Nothing in his analysis suggests that Dad might rightly hear Mom's "Only two more days till Christmas" as the announcement that she has just won the lottery and he will soon be driving that long-coveted Porsche. With explicit reference to Hirsch, Ricoeur writes:

> If it is true that there is always more than one way of construing a text, it is not true that all interpretations are equal. . . . The text is a limited field of possible construction. . . . It is always possible to argue for or against an interpretation, to confront interpretations, to arbitrate between them, and to seek for an agreement, even if this agreement remains beyond our reach. (*HHS* 213)

Ricoeur's hermeneutics develops a dialectic of belonging and distanciation. By belonging he means the embeddedness of (human) author and reader alike in contingent and particular horizons, contexts, and perspectives to which the meanings they put or find in a text are relative. It is because the six blind men "belong" to the positions in which they find themselves that (1) they have access and insight into the elephant at all and (2) that their access is finite and incomplete. By distanciation Ricoeur means the adoption of methods of testing interpretations that render the reader as objective as possible and that treat the text as an object to be explained. The methods of math and physics are in the background, methods in which the "interpreter" seeks to neutralize personal perspectives for the sake of universal, transcultural objectivity. These methods make possible what Derrida calls "doubling commentary" and what Gadamer calls the "reproductive" dimension of interpretation.[19] Most of Ricoeur's discussion of distanciation revolves around structuralism, which hovered over French thought as an inescapable influence during his lifetime. At times he seems, unfortunately, almost to identify distanciation with structuralist strategies for reading. Fortunately, we do not need to concern ourselves with this theory, which no longer dominates the French intellectual scene and has never dominated the Anglo-American scene. For the theologian, grammatical-historical exegesis is closer to home. It involves scholarly norms by which biblical interpreters seek to step back, to distance themselves from the particularities of the traditions to which they "belong."

Like Derrida, Ricoeur thinks that objectifying methods are an indispensable "guardrail" to interpretation, a necessary protection against lapsing into an "anything goes" attitude. But he also thinks they should not be the tail wagging the dog. To make the text an object to be explained with the help of some method for the sake of objectivism in interpretation and to identify this task as the whole hermeneutical task is to treat the text like "a cadaver handed over for autopsy" and to act "as though one were to give the funeral eulogy of someone yet alive. The eulogy might be accurate and appropriate, but it is nonetheless 'premature,' as Mark Twain might have put it."[20]

19. See *HHS* 43, 60–61, 74, 92, 116, 131, 154, 209–10, 217.

20. In André LaCocque and Paul Ricoeur, *Thinking Biblically: Exegetical and Hermeneutical Studies*, trans. David Pellauer (Chicago: University of Chicago Press, 1998), xii. See also Dietrich Bonhoeffer's claim that historical-critical interpretation of the Bible "left behind nothing but 'dust and ashes'" (see Eberhard Bethge, *Dietrich Bonhoeffer: Theologian, Christian, Contemporary*, trans. Edwin Robertson et al. [London: Collins, 1970], 56–57). Bonhoeffer also recognized a role for objectifying methods, though it was a subordinate one.

6

Rehabilitating Tradition

It is finally time to turn to Hans-Georg Gadamer's hermeneutics as developed in *Truth and Method*, the most influential twentieth-century work in philosophical hermeneutics. It is not an easy text. It is sometimes said that one is not prepared to read any serious philosophical text until one has already read it at least once, and there is a lot of truth in this reminder that philosophy, like physics, takes serious, disciplined preparation. There are no cheap seats where the love of wisdom reigns. In the present case the preparation, minimal to be sure, has been a brief overview of the development of philosophical hermeneutics since Schleiermacher and a sketch of some recent debates. Gadamer's magnum opus covers the same territory in a comprehensive and relatively systematic manner, so we turn to his work not entirely unprepared for what we will encounter there.

Like Schleiermacher, Gadamer seeks to develop a "deregionalized" theory of interpretation. While he makes explicit reference to literary, legal, and theological interpretation, he intends his theory to apply to the reading of all culturally significant texts. Moreover, he emphasizes that his is a descriptive, rather than normative, theory of interpretation. It is not a how-to-do-it manual spelling out rules for "validity in interpretation" but an attempt to see clearly what happens when we interpret so as to understand "works."[1] *Truth and*

---

1. Gadamer makes friendly reference to Heidegger's extension of interpretation beyond texts to all "objects" of cognition, but he focuses on "works," that is, texts

Method is not a discourse on method. "My real concern was and is philosophic: not what we do or what we ought to do, but what happens to us over and above our wanting and doing."[2]

What happens to us is, in a word, tradition: our "thrownness" into it,[3] our immersion in it, and our formation by it. If the term "formation" evokes the concept of spiritual formation (conversion as an ongoing process), splendid. For what is at issue is not merely the addition or subtraction of certain propositions from the list of those we would affirm, if asked; it is rather the process by which we come to see and to feel and thus to act in harmony with what we purport to believe.

The Fundamental Thesis about Tradition: Belonging

This thesis has just been stated. We belong to tradition by virtue of our thrownness into it, our immersion in it, and our formation by it. This is an ontological claim about our being and an epistemological claim about our understanding of ourselves and our world. Because we are

> situated within traditions . . . history does not belong to us; we belong to it. Long before we understand ourselves through the process of self-examination, we understand ourselves in a self-evident way in the family, society, and state [and, we might add, church] in which we live. . . . *That is why the prejudices [Vorurteile] of the individual, far more than his judgments [Urteile], constitute the historical reality of his being.* (TM 276–77/277–78)[4]

---

and works of nonverbal art as public and relatively permanent bearers of culturally significant meaning.

2. Hans-Georg Gadamer, *Truth and Method*, trans. Joel Weinsheimer and Donald G. Marshall, 2nd ed. (New York: Crossroad, 1989, 2004), xxi–xxiii/xxii and xxviii/xxvi. In a reader-unfriendly gesture, Crossroad reissued this second edition in 2004 with different pagination. Citations in text and notes will be as follows: *TM* x/y, where x = pagination for the 1989 edition and y = pagination for the 2004 edition.

3. On thrownness as a formal character of human existence, see Martin Heidegger, *Being and Time*, trans. John Macquarrie and Edward Robinson (New York: Harper, 1962), 38. The basic point is that we find ourselves immersed in and formed by traditions we have not chosen.

4. Note that what often appears to us to be self-evident and thus immediate (intuition rather than interpretation) is seen here as richly mediated by prior interpretations. Remember the racist from chap. 1 who "just sees" the inferiority of those different from "us."

There are three things to notice here. First, tradition plays a double role. By giving us a place to stand, it plays an enabling role. It makes interpretation and understanding possible. In Kantian language, it is "the condition of possible experience." We would have to be either God or dead not to stand in some such particular and contingent place, and in neither case would human understanding be possible. At the same time, our location limits us to what can be seen from that perspective. By placing us where we can grasp the elephant's tail, it puts us in a position from which we cannot see the trunk.

Second, "traditions" is plural. We are not formed by a single, coherently univocal tradition. Just as the Ohio River is formed by the confluence of the Monongahela and the Allegheny rivers, so we are born and bred by the confluence of many streams of tradition. Moreover, this plurality applies to both the theological and the secular traditions by which nurture has become second nature in us. For example, just as I was born of German, Dutch, and English stock but in the United States, so my earliest religious formation drew on Lutheran, Calvinist, Baptist, Congregational, pietist, and dispensational traditions.

Third, the result of our belonging to tradition is prejudice. Gadamer uses the term in its etymological sense: pre-judgment. By virtue of our belonging, tradition produces within us the a priori element in interpretation. The double result is that all interpretation is perspectival and no interpretation is presuppositionless. Here we meet again our old friend the hermeneutical circle, in which every interpretation is guided by some preunderstanding. Since Gadamer has had the courage to use that scary word "prejudice," we can take our courage in hand and say that this is a relativist hermeneutics: all interpretation is relative to traditions that have formed the perspectives and presuppositions that guide it.[5] But, of course, this not to say that "anything goes," that all perspectives are equally illuminating. Looking at an amoeba through a telescope will not prove very satisfying.

Still, there is something scary about this talk of prejudice and relativity. Hence the question raised by Dilthey, "But where are the

5. The locations that constitute the perspectives and presuppositions from which interpretation emerges have gone by many different names in twentieth-century philosophy, such as: horizons, life-worlds, language games, practices, modes of being-in-the-world, *Weltanschauungen*, society, and culture.

means to overcome the anarchy of opinions that then threatens to befall us?" (see chap. 2). The comforting thought might occur that we might be able to escape the power of our prejudices by becoming conscious of them. But Gadamer rejects this suggestion. "*To be historically means that knowledge of oneself can never be complete.* All self-knowledge arises from what is historically pregiven. . . . We are concerned to conceive a reality that limits and exceeds the omnipotence of reflection" (*TM* 302/301, 342/338; emphasis in the original).

Our immersion in tradition is like trying to look at a Monet or a Jackson Pollock painting from twelve inches away. We can't really grasp what we do see, and part of the large painting is beyond our horizon of vision. The solution, of course, is to stand back and view the painting from a distance at which we can grasp the whole. Then those little globs of paint become so much more than that as they resolve themselves into the Japanese foot bridge or an even more abstract expression of mood or movement or color. The objectivist idea is that in reflection we can stand back, neutralize the limits of that original perspective, and grasp the whole apart from any such limits.

Gadamer's claim is that this is impossible, that while we can move from one perspective to another and can stand back and broaden our horizons in the process, this very process is an always-unfinished task. Put in Dilthey's language, what we want to understand is life (or history). But, according to Gadamer, we are immersed in life (or history) and can never stand back from life (or history) and view it as a whole. Total distanciation is never possible.

We can understand as a double difficulty the claim that full transparency through reflection is not possible. We can never become fully conscious of our prejudices because every effort at such self-examination will itself be guided by presuppositions not yet brought to reflective transparency, and even when we become aware of aspects of our formation, these elements do not stop working but continue to do so, often behind our backs. Thus, for example, I know (perspectivally, and thus in part) that I have been formed by the media that are part of my daily experience, but I can scarcely claim that this knowledge keeps them from shaping my life in ways that I don't fully notice or, for that matter, approve.

Gadamer has an interesting set of responses to Dilthey's question and to Hirsch's attempt to answer it. But first we need to take a closer look at what he says about tradition. The remaining theses can be thought of as corollaries, caveats, or contextualizations of the central thesis about belonging.

Not Quite Ninety-Five Corollary Theses about Tradition

The Alterity Thesis

The texts and other works that tradition has handed down to us are not so much objects over which we exercise mastery as they are voices to which we do well to listen. They speak; they address us; they make claims on us. Hence the reference to alterity, the otherness that is not just part of the world as defined by us but different enough to put us and that world in question. Like the Little League coach who says, "Swing Hard. You might hit it," so Gadamer says, "Listen carefully. You might learn something. The voice you hear is not your own, but one that from a different perspective makes a truth claim on you."[6] Echoing journalist Walter Cronkite, it says, "And that's the way it is."

Of course, our listening and thus our interpreting will be shaped by the traditions that have formed us. What tradition sets *before* us will be understood in terms of what tradition has already done *within* us. But those traditions themselves are more nearly voices than inert and impersonal causes. They are like our parents and teachers.[7] In the process of socialization we may internalize our parents' and teachers' beliefs, attitudes, and practices, but socialization is never complete, and they never cease to be a voice other than our own. So to seek to neutralize their impact in its totality is to try to silence the alterity of two voices, that of tradition and that of the text, which are themselves a confluence of traditions. We will not be able to hear anything that surprises us or challenges us but only what we already take to be self-evident.

6. It is no accident that one of the best books on Gadamer is titled *Hermeneutics and the Voice of the Other* by James Risser (Albany: SUNY Press, 1997). Cf. *TM* 14/12, 17/15.

7. In Plato's *Crito*, 50d–51e, Socrates describes the laws of Athens as his parents and teachers. In his notion of *Sittlichkeit*, usually translated as "ethical life," Hegel expands this to include the laws and customs of one's people. It is the background against which parents can sometimes be heard justifying a prohibition by saying, "We don't do that" or "We don't do things that way."

The Authority Thesis

The claim here is quite simple: tradition exercises authority in/ over our thinking, our construals, and our seeings as. This is both a de facto and a de jure claim. As a matter of observable fact, traditions shape our interpretations and the resulting understandings. We are *wirkungsgeschichtliches Bewusstsein*. This term is an arrow to have in one's quiver, for in the middle of a debate in which one doesn't know what else to say, one can silence the opponent by saying, "But you aren't taking seriously enough your status as *wirkungsgeschichtliches Bewusstsein*." The term simply means "historically effected consciousness."[8] My consciousness is not a transparent, self-grounding vehicle that puts me in immediate contact with its "object" but is rather a grounded opacity (or at best a translucency) that enables a richly mediated contact with its "object."

If we doubt the fact alluded to here, we do well to remind ourselves of the history of Christian doctrine and of our friends the desert fathers, the Geneva Calvinists, the American slaves, and today's Amish. God does indeed work in mysterious ways, but it would be passing strange if the Holy Spirit guided everyone else to "truth" relative to and thus limited by a particular perspective and gave only to "us" the privilege of an unmediated, pure, objective access to *the truth*. To claim that God speaks to us in revelation is one thing. To claim that God gives us a God's-eye view of revelation's meaning, thereby transforming us from human to divine knowers, is quite another. Like the French "death of the author" writers, Gadamer uses theological language when speaking about the finitude of historically effected consciousness. What we need is "insight into the limitations of humanity, into the absoluteness of the barrier that separates man from the divine" (*TM* 357/351).

The authority thesis is also a de jure claim. The traditions that have shaped us have a right to our respect. They have always already functioned like our parents and teachers. If we think of teenagers who want to free themselves from anything and everything their parents have taught them or now say to them, we can see how the attempt to reflect ourselves out of any dependence on tradition is a matter of both arrogance and ingratitude. Back to Logic 101: the discovery that parental traditions are finite and fallible is not the

8. See the sustained analysis in *TM* 300–307/299–306 and 341–79/336–71.

discovery (1) that they are always wrong or (2) that we ourselves are somehow infinite and infallible.

The Fallibility Thesis

So then, the authority of tradition is real but not absolute. In terms of the de facto authority, it is always possible to relocate, to open ourselves to be influenced by other traditions and thus re-formed. Even if, on Gadamer's view, we can never realize the Enlightenment ideal—expressed so confidently by Descartes and Locke at the birth of modernity—of escaping the locating power of tradition altogether, we are not, as *wirkungsgeschichtliches Bewusstsein*, imprisoned in any particular location. In terms of the de jure authority, we can and should recognize the fallibility of tradition. For it, too, is finite and human, all too human, and never immune to critique.

The prejudices we inherit from tradition are at once the conditions of possible experience and its limits. There are "legitimate prejudices" (*TM* 277/278) and "enabling prejudices" (*TM* 295/295). But we cannot avoid the question of critique, "namely how to distinguish the true prejudices, by which we *understand*, from the *false* ones, by which we *misunderstand*" (*TM* 298–99/298). Actually, it's not that simple in Gadamer's view. The difference between "true" (legitimate, enabling) and "false" (illegitimate, misleading) prejudices is not a neat either/or but more nearly a matter of degree. Different presuppositions are more or less illuminating, more or less blinding. As with Schleiermacher, working back and forth within the hermeneutical circle is always "provisional and unending" (*TM* 190/189). The hope is always to work from misunderstanding to greater understanding, but there is no resting place where the simply true prejudice has resulted in the final and definitive understanding.

Gadamer writes:

A person who is trying to understand a text is always projecting. He projects a meaning for the text as a whole as soon as some initial meaning emerges in the text. . . . Working out this fore-projection [prejudice], which is constantly *revised* in terms of what emerges as he penetrates into the meaning, is understanding what is there. . . . The process that Heidegger describes [in terms of the hermeneutical circle] is that every *revision* of the fore-projection is capable of projecting before itself a new projection of meaning; rival projects can emerge side by side until it becomes clearer what the unity of meaning is; interpretation begins with fore-conceptions that are *replaced* by more suitable ones. This *constant process* of new projection constitutes the movement of understanding and interpretation. (*TM* 267/269; emphases added)

Revise. Revise. Replace. This is the finitude and fallibility of human understanding, the limit to the authority of tradition. There is no Alpha point (a la Descartes) that can serve as an absolute foundation, immune to revision and replacement. Nor is there any Omega point (a la Hegel) that brings the process to a definitive conclusion, also immune to revision and replacement. The process, according to Gadamer, is "constant." We are always *in medias res* or, as the Germans love to say, *unterwegs*.

Once again we are reminded of the plain fact that the interpretation of the Constitution, of Shakespeare, and of the Bible keeps on keeping on. What Gadamer says of the work of art he extends to all interpretation: "There is no absolute progress and no final exhaustion of what lies in a work of art" (*TM* 100/87). We shall see in due course why the work of art is so important to Gadamer's theory of interpretation, but there is a more immediate concern to which we must turn.

7

On Not Clinging to the Prejudice against Prejudice

Why the Author Can't Rescue Us from the Reader's Relativity

Gadamer's treatise on tradition underscores the relativity of the reader to a historically effected perspective that evokes the vertigo of relativity and Dilthey's anxiety about anarchy, for different readers (and communities of readers) belong to and are shaped by different traditions. This brings us back to the alleged privilege of the author that has occupied us in chapters 4 and 5. Might the author's (intended) meaning provide hermeneutics with a *determinate object* (THE meaning of the text) that by means of intuition (divination, as Schleiermacher puts it) and *methodical validation* can preserve objectivity in the sense of universal validity for interpretation?

Gadamer thinks not. To think this way is to cling to what he calls the prejudice against prejudice. As he sees it, "there is one prejudice of the Enlightenment [i.e., "modernity," in much contemporary discourse] that defines its essence: the fundamental prejudice of the Enlightenment is the prejudice against prejudice itself, which denies tradition its power [both de facto and de jure]" (*TM* 270/272–73). Like Ricoeur, Gadamer seeks to loosen the grip of this prejudice against prejudice and to quash the hope, which he views as illusory, that by appeal to authorial authority we can neutralize the effects of tradition. He minces no words:

> Every age has to understand a transmitted text in its own way. . . . The real meaning of a text, as it speaks to the interpreter, does not depend on the contingencies of the author and his original audience. It certainly is not identical with them, for it is always *co-determined* [emphasis added] also by the historical situation of the interpreter. . . . Not just occasionally but always, the text goes beyond its author. That is why understanding is not merely a reproductive but always a productive activity as well. . . . It is enough to say that we understand in a *different* way, *if we understand at all*. (*TM* 296–97/296; cf. 395/396–97)

Or again:

> It is part of the historical finitude of our being that we are aware that others after us will understand in a different way. And yet it is equally indubitable that it remains the same work whose fullness of meaning is realized in the changing process of understanding, just as it is the same history whose meaning is constantly in the process of being defined. The hermeneutical reduction to the author's meaning is just as inappropriate as the reduction of historical events to the intentions of their protagonists. (*TM* 373/366)

The point about historical events is being illustrated even as this chapter is being written. The significance of the war in Iraq, begun in 2003, is vastly different from what was intended by President George W. Bush and his neocon supporters when they started it. One might say that they have produced both more and less than they intended. The strength of the analogy Gadamer draws between historical agency and authorial production can be seen in a helpful essay on his delimitation of authorial authority. Two sections of that essay are titled "Less in the Text Than the Author Intended" and "More in the Text Than the Author Intended."[1]

Like Wolterstorff and Ricoeur, Gadamer rejects the psychologism of Schleiermacher[2] and Dilthey. He rejects the expressivist view of

---

1. David Weberman, "Gadamer's Hermeneutics and the Question of Authorial Intention," in *The Death and Resurrection of the Author?* ed. William Irwin (Westport, CT: Greenwood, 2002), 45–64.

2. At least sometimes. See chap. 2, note 11.

language and the notion that interpretation reverses the process of authorial production by recreating or reconstructing and thus repeating the creative event by transposing ourselves into the mind of the author (*TM* 133/129, 159/152). His reason is not so much that this is impossible but that most of the time it is not what we are looking for. Unless we're writing a biography, we don't read the text as its author's autobiography. If the text is a voice to be heard (a Thou) and not an object to be mastered (an It), what we seek to understand "is not the Thou but the truth of what the Thou says to us" (*TM* xxxv/xxxii). Psychologism and its expressivist view of language holds that the interpreter "regards the texts, independently of their claim to truth, as purely expressive phenomena. . . . Neither the saving truth of Scripture nor the exemplariness of the classics was to influence a procedure that was able to grasp every text as an expression of life and ignore the truth of what was said" (*TM* 196–97/194–95). Or again:

> When we try to understand a text, we do not try to transpose ourselves into the author's mind but, if one wants to use this terminology, we try to transpose ourselves into the perspective within which he has formed his views. But this simply means that we try to understand how what he is saying could be right. . . . The task of hermeneutics is to clarify this miracle of understanding, which is not a mysterious communion of souls, but sharing in a public meaning. (*TM* 292/292)

We can put this once again in the language of discourse theory. Discourse (spoken or written) occurs when someone says something about something to someone. Against the assumption that in interpretation what we seek to understand is that first someone, Gadamer, like Wolterstorff and Ricoeur, claims that what we typically want to understand is that something about something. Gadamer emphasizes that it's about the truth claim of the text, what it offers as the truth about its subject matter. In other words, we seek to understand the something said (meaning) in order to understand that about which it is said (truth).

At this point we need to remind ourselves that there is an appeal to authorial authority for the sake of objectivity that survives the dismissal of psychologism. The idea, we can recall, was to allow the author to fix the meaning of the text so as to neutralize the relativizing effect of many readers in many different contexts. Might this still be possible, even when we have shifted hermeneutical attention from the inner life of the author to the public content of the authorial speech act? If the something about something becomes the "object" to be understood, might its *content* be fixed and determinate enough and our mode of *access* to it methodical or rule-governed enough to retain objectivity or universal validity in interpretation?

Consider the case of a common form of pig Latin. Mom wants to ask Dad a question that the kids won't understand. "Allshay eeway ohgay ootay acmay onaldsday?" Dad has no trouble understanding this as the question, "Shall we go to McDonald's?" His interpreting is an act of deciphering, reproductive without being productive. In the first place, the meaning is sufficiently determinate that it neither requires nor permits input from Dad. Mom has put a fixed meaning into play, and anyone who understands this version of pig Latin, including the readers of this chapter, will understand it in the same way as Mom intended it and Dad interprets it. The reason for this unanimity is that all of them (the different "readers") have a method, a rule-governed procedure, for decoding or deciphering Mom's already-fixed meaning. The ideal of hermeneutical objectivity is realized because (1) the content is (sufficiently) determinate as determined by the author, and (2) the readers are in possession of a method or mode of access that neutralizes the differences among them.

Some "readers" will be big fans of McDonald's. Others will much prefer Wendy's. Still others will be against fast food in general because of its use of trans fats and their cardiological effects. Still others will be against fast food simply because of what it does to their waistlines. But these differences will be hermeneutically irrelevant. They will all get the same meaning from Mom's question.

Once again, Gadamer says no—emphatically—to this model for hermeneutics. Interpreting is not deciphering for two reasons, one concerning the *content* and one concerning the mode of *access* or method. Regarding the content, his claim is that the author alone cannot render the text sufficiently determinate because the author is not fully in charge of the creation of meaning. Remembering that Gadamer assimilates texts to nontextual works of art, we read, "Works of art are detached from their origins and, just because of this, begin to speak—perhaps *surprising even their creators*."[3]

3. Hans-Georg Gadamer, "Hermeneutics and Logocentrism," in *Dialogue and Deconstruction: The Gadamer-Derrida Encounter*, ed. Diane P. Michelfelder and Richard E. Palmer (Albany: SUNY Press, 1989), 123; emphasis added.

There are at least two reasons for thinking this way. First, the author, too, is *wirkungsgeschichtliches Bewusstsein*, lacking the self-transparency to know in any absolute way what the work says (*TM* 133/129). In creating the text, the author is not like God creating the world, so the text does not contain all and only what the author (intended to) put in it. It contains both more and less than that. Second, Gadamer appeals to the idea of genius as developed by Kant and the German romantics. It converts into a theory the idea of the poet inspired by a muse or a prophet inspired by God. The idea is simply that there is a power at work in finite authorial creation—for Gadamer the power of tradition—of whose agency and effects the author is never fully aware. So this second point is the first point expressed in a slightly different manner.[4]

In this way of thinking there is an unconscious dimension of the author's work that is much stronger than that presented by Hirsch (chap. 4). An implication of this is that the author is also a reader of the text, and not necessarily a privileged one. In the context of genius theory, Gadamer writes of the author:

> As an interpreter he has no automatic authority over the person who is simply receiving his work. Insofar as he reflects on his own work, he is his own reader. . . . Thus the idea of production by genius performs an important theoretical task, in that it collapses the distinction between interpreter and author. (*TM* 193/192)

This is not to say that the distinction disappears completely. But the difference is compromised so as to deprive the author of the godlike ability to produce a fixed and final meaning, leaving to the reader only the task of deciphering it. The pesky reader won't go away quietly.

The essential role of the reader is expressed in the passage cited above, which states that meaning is "codetermined" by author and reader. For Gadamer, this is an ontological claim about the work. The text or work of art by itself is indeterminate and incomplete. In other words, "understanding belongs to the being of that which is understood" (*TM* xxxi/xxviii; cf. 164/157). The work is an "*unfin-*

4. Gadamer might have strengthened his case for the opacity of authorial consciousness by appealing to the psychoanalytic model of Freud, the ideological model of Marx, and the genealogical model of Nietzsche. See Merold Westphal, *Suspicion and Faith: The Religious Uses of Modern Atheism* (New York: Fordham University Press, 1998).

ished event" (*TM* 99/85). If we are talking about a play, the spectator belongs to it essentially (*TM* 116, 128, 130/115, 125–26). If we
are talking about a text, it is the reader who is essential. "The text
[that the author produced] brings a subject matter into language,
but that it does so is ultimately the achievement of the interpreter.
Both have a share in it" (*TM* 388/390).

(Note that there are two crucial but different senses of belonging
in Gadamer's hermeneutics. The interpreter belongs to the traditions
that make up the home and horizon from which interpretation arises
and to which it is relative. The interpreter also belongs to the text or
work that is interpreted as the codeterminer of its meaning.)

There is that old conundrum about the tree falling in the woods
with no one to hear it. Is there any sound? Gadamer, it seems,
would say, "No!" There would only be the vibration of air waves
(or something like that). For there to be sound there would have to
be someone with the power of hearing that could interpret those air
waves as this or that sound. Of course, without the air waves there
could be no sound. Hearing is a combination of reproduction and
production. So the birth of the reader is not the absolute death of
the author but only the death of the absolute author, the one who
could fix meaning unilaterally. –

Why Method Can't Rescue Us from the Reader's Relativity

If the *content* of authorial discourse does not lend itself to an objectivist hermeneutics, neither can the appeal to a method or mode of
access do the job. The first reason has already been given. As Hirsch
has made clear, such a hermeneutics requires a fixed and final object,
his candidate being, of course, the author's intended meaning. But
if the author can produce only a meaning that is incomplete as it
emerges in the text, method will not be able to supply the desired
determinacy.

But Gadamer has more to say about method than this. It has often
been said that his title should have been *Truth against Method*. There
is a good deal of truth in this, because, as we shall see, he wants to
affirm a truth beyond the reach and control of method. But it is
also misleading, because he doesn't embody an unqualified hostility toward being "scientific" by seeking truth within the reach and
control of method. Insofar as interpretation is reproductive, there

is room for method. But insofar as interpretation is productive as
well, there is, he claims, a truth beyond method. So perhaps the title
might have been *Truth beyond Method*. In his opening paragraph
Gadamer writes, "Even from its historical beginnings, the problem
of hermeneutics goes *beyond* the limits of the concept of method as
set by modern science." Hermeneutics is "*not merely*" a matter of
science, "is *not basically* a problem of method at all. . . . It is *not concerned primarily* with amassing verified knowledge, such as would
satisfy the methodological ideal of science" (*TM* xxi/xx; emphasis
added). The qualifiers "merely," "basically," and "primarily" leave
open a space for method to play a subordinate role. But it cannot
be the tail that wags the dog. Accordingly, Gadamer insists that his
book is not a treatise on method (*TM* xxiii/xxii, xxxvi/xxxiii).

Two of Gadamer's most significant comments on the methodological ideal of the natural sciences come in relation to Hermann Helmholtz and our friend Wilhelm Dilthey. Helmholtz was an anatomist,
physicist, and physiologist who gave a famous lecture in 1862 on the
relation between the natural sciences and the human sciences.[5] He
held the latter to be epistemically inferior because they did not live
up to the methodological objectivity of the former. To this Gadamer
replies, "For Helmholtz the methodological ideal of the natural sciences needed neither to be historically derived nor epistemologically
restricted, and that is why he could not understand the way the human
sciences work as logically different" (*TM* 6/5).

To say that this ideal, which Dilthey and Hirsch want to incorpo-
rate into hermeneutics, is "historically derived" is to say two things
that Helmholtz overlooked. First, this ideal has a history. It did not
drop straight down from heaven but emerged in history at certain
times and places and under certain circumstances. It is not and has
not been the only understanding of knowledge and truth that the
human race has had. It is one way among others, and its right to
colonial hegemony over all others is not self-evident. Second, this
history, including the belief that this is the mode of knowing by
which all others are to be measured, is itself a tradition, the one
that "denies tradition its power [both de facto and de jure]" (*TM*

---

5. "Human sciences" is the standard translation of *Geisteswissenschaften*, the sciences of spirit as distinct from nature. They comprise what we call the social sciences
and the humanities, including legal theory, literary criticism, and theology. Dilthey's
project was to find a "separate but equal" objectivity for the human sciences.

270/272–73). The irony is obvious. Modernity invokes this tradition that would free us from tradition but that, as a tradition itself,
undermines its own aspirations.

Further, to say that this ideal is "epistemologically restricted"
is to say that this mode of knowing enables us to see things we
couldn't see without it but at the same time cuts us off from things
we can discover only through other modes of knowing. Like the six
blind men from Hindustan (chap. 1) or like using a microscope or
like looking at a Monet or Jackson Pollock painting from twelve
inches away (chap. 6). One can notice or discover truths otherwise
not available but at the cost of not seeing truths available only from
other perspectives. Thus "epistemological restriction" has two meanings: the posture of methodological objectivism restricts our vision
as well as expands it, and we need to restrict our claims about its
importance accordingly, taking fully into account both what it can
and what it cannot do.

The other important comment about method comes when Gadamer cites Dilthey's obituary for Wilhelm Scherer, who was much
enamored with the objectivity of the natural sciences in relation to
historical research. Dilthey writes, "He was a *modern* man, and the
world of our forebears was no longer the *home* of his spirit and his
heart, but his historical *object*" (emphasis added). To this Gadamer
replies, "The antithesis shows that for Dilthey scientific knowledge
obliges one to sever one's bond with life, to attain distance from
one's own history, which alone makes it possible for that history to
become an object" (*TM* 7/6).

Once again Gadamer is making two points. First, he is not denying
either the possibility or the usefulness of a certain distanciation or
objectification. This is where Derrida's "instruments of traditional
criticism" (methods, if you like) in the service of "doubling commentary" come in to serve as a "guardrail" (chap. 5) along with Gadamer's own account of interpretation as "reproductive." But second,
he insists that while we can adopt postures and employ methods
that enable us to step back from our most immediate immersion in
tradition, this distanciation can never be complete for the simple
reason that it occurs within a particular tradition-al location. It is
in belonging to our history that we are able to distance ourselves
from it *to the degree* that this is possible.

This possibility is limited because it is "one's own history alone
that makes it possible for that history [or the text that belongs to

a particular history] to become an object" for us. One reason is that we never completely free ourselves from our prejudices, as anyone who follows the debates in biblical scholarship can easily see. The other reason is that, as already mentioned, the move to method for the sake of objectivity is itself a tradition that has become part of our history.[6] Whereas Ricoeur warns that in distanciation, which he strongly affirms, we run the risk of turning the text and its subject matter into a "cadaver handed over for autopsy" (chap. 5) and thus *should* never separate distanciation from belonging, Gadamer's point is that we *couldn't* do this even if we tried, though if we persuade ourselves that we have done so we may end up giving "the funeral eulogy of someone yet alive" (chap. 5).

It isn't just that methodological distanciation can never be complete. The dilemma is also that it puts us in a problematic relation to the text, seeking to dominate by subordinating it to our procedures rather than being willing "to open ourselves to the superior claim the text makes and to respond to what it has to tell us . . . subordinating ourselves to the text's claim to dominate our minds" (*TM* 311/310; cf. 360–61/354–55). This is not a servile capitulation to any text we happen to come on. To speak of the "superior claim" of the text is simply to obey the injunction, "Listen carefully. You might learn something" (chap. 6). It is to hope, even to expect, that the text will illumine its subject matter for us from a perspective we haven't yet occupied.

How are we to relieve Dilthey's despair and Hirsch's hysteria? Not, according to Gadamer, by clinging to objectivist hopes with the help of both an author who can unilaterally produce determinate meaning and a quasi-scientific method that will enable us to decipher that already-fixed and final meaning from some (non)standpoint of neutral objectivity.[7]

Emilio Betti is a kindred spirit to Dilthey and Hirsch, so we will not be surprised to find him unsatisfied at this point. Gadamer's problem, as he sees it, is that he allows meaning to occur

6. Thus in biblical studies, e.g., the methods of form criticism, redaction criticism, comparative anthropology, and so forth are themselves particular traditions that are both "historically derived" and "epistemologically restricted," not least because of the presuppositions involved in their use.

7. On the link between interpretation as deciphering and language as expression, see *TM* 241/234.

without, however, *guaranteeing* the *correctness* of understanding; for that it would be necessary that the understanding arrived at *corresponded* fully to the meaning of the underlying text as an objectivation of mind. Only then would the *objectivity* of the result be *guaranteed* on the basis of a reliable process of interpretation. It can easily be demonstrated that the proposed method cannot claim to achieve objectivity.[8]

It is instructive that in a passage this short Betti should twice raise the demand for guarantees. No doubt all of us some of the time and some of us all of the time would like guarantees that we're the ones who have gotten it right. But it does not follow either that we need such guarantees or that they are available. Betti's demand helps us to understand Gadamer's hermeneutics as a sustained argument that we do not need and cannot have such guarantees. Of course, Gadamer would immediately agree that his "proposed method cannot claim to achieve objectivity," if only he had proposed a method rather than arguing against the possibility of method as the sure path to scientific objectivity.

But Gadamer realizes that his case for truth beyond method is incomplete. Against objectivist appeals to authorial privilege and methodological guarantees, he has argued for the essential role of the reader and the situated relativity of that reader. But these are negative arguments against central claims of objectivist hermeneutics. In sports and politics we say that you can't beat anybody with nobody. We need a fuller, positive picture of what Gadamer proposes as an alternative. He knows this, and in his opening paragraph he poses the question that now arises for us: "In understanding tradition not only are texts understood, but insights are acquired and truths known. But what kind of knowledge and what kind of truth?" (*TM* xxi/xx). We can now turn to his answer to his own question.

---

8. Emilio Betti, "Hermeneutics as the General Methodology of the *Geisteswissenschaften*," in *Contemporary Hermeneutics: Hermeneutics as Method, Philosophy, and Critique*, ed. Josef Bleicher (London: Routledge and Kegan Paul, 1980), 79; emphasis added.

8

Art as the Site of Truth
beyond Method

The Humanist Tradition

Over against the "romantic" idea of interpretation as the attempt to re-create or reconstruct the inner life of the author, reversing the process of linguistic expression, Gadamer sets the idea of interpretation as the search for the truth of what the author says about the *Sache*, the subject matter of the discourse. And over against the idea that the only path to truth is some scientific method aimed at and in principle capable of achieving objective, that is, universally valid, results, he sets the idea that there is truth beyond method. We know from what has already been said that interpretation will be the mode of access to this truth, but to understand what this means we'll have to answer Gadamer's own question: what kind of truth?

The primary answer Gadamer gives to this question is the truth of art, so he turns our attention to the humanistic tradition that seeks truth beyond method by means of interpreting classic texts and works of art (*TM* xxii/xxi). Gadamer contrasts the humanistic tradition with the now dominant scientific tradition. By the latter, Gadamer understands not merely the natural sciences, whose impact on Western culture since Copernicus,

Galileo, and Newton has been incalculable;[1] his special focus is on the attempt to extend scientific method to the human "sciences" (*Geisteswissenschaften*)[2] so as to neutralize tradition and its "prejudices." We have already seen that this is Dilthey's project, namely, to develop a method for historical research that will yield universal validity. In this, Dilthey is responding to a development in nineteenth-century German historiography whose insistence on its scientific objectivity is nicely summed up in Leopold von Ranke's notion that the historian's narratives give us the past just as it actually happened (*wie es eigentlich gewesen*).[3] In other words, just like Sgt. Friday of *Dragnet* fame, who wanted "Just the facts, ma'am," the historian seeks, and in principle succeeds, in providing a mirror image of historical events. No interpretation needed! No need to worry about the "anarchy of opinions" (chap. 2). Dilthey's project was to show just how this was possible.

Already in the eighteenth century, David Hume had traveled boldly along this path. He subtitled his *A Treatise of Human Nature* with this astonishing aspiration: *BEING an Attempt to Introduce the Experimental Method of Reasoning* INTO MORAL SUBJECTS. The experimental method he had in mind is that with which Copernicus, Kepler, Galileo, and especially Newton had given birth to the scientific revolution that became the heart of modernity. The "moral" subjects Hume then proceeded to discuss included epistemology, psychology, and ethics.

Over against this scientism, the humanism to which Gadamer appeals seeks to find truth beyond method in classic texts and works

1. Thus Alexander Pope famously writes in his epitaph for Newton:
> Nature and Nature's laws lay hid in night:
> God said, Let Newton be! and all was light.

2. Notice how language itself is a tradition. The German term, literally "sciences of spirit," begs a crucial question by suggesting that not only what we call the social sciences but even what we call the humanities are to be thought of as sciences, which presumably ought to be "scientific." Our term "social sciences" does the same for a subset of the *Geisteswissenschaften*, so it is not surprising that in our universities the study of economics, politics, and social relations is overwhelmingly quantitative and experimental, as much like physics as possible. Once this project is carried out in microeconomics, the latter becomes the model for rational choice theory and thus for the redefinition of reason in terms of measuring, calculating, and predicting in the service of one's interests.

3. Grammar requires that this phrase be concluded with an *ist*, but Ranke gave himself the (un)poetic license to omit it.

of art, understood not as objects to be observed and explained but as voices to be listened to. David Tracy's definition of a classic text is entirely in tune with Gadamer's understanding. Classics are:

> those texts that have helped found or form a particular culture . . . those texts that bear an excess and permanence of meaning, yet always resist definitive interpretation. In their production, there is also the following paradox: though highly particular in origin and expression, classics have the possibility of being universal in their effect.[4]

Gadamer is thinking especially of the cultural importance of the literary heritage of Greco-Roman antiquity as it emerged particularly in the Renaissance, continued through the Enlightenment (as a parallel track to its growing worship of science), and continued on to his own personal formation. The humanist tradition looked for truth beyond method in such places as the tragedies of Aeschylus and Sophocles; the epics of Homer and Virgil; the histories of Herodotus, Thucydides, Tacitus, and Julius Caesar; and the philosophical treatises of Plato, Aristotle, and the Stoics.

Gadamer also includes works of art, not all of which are literary. Here we need to think about two partially overlapping circles (what logicians call a Venn diagram). One is labeled LW for literary work and the other WA for work of art. In the area where the two overlap we have literary works of art. In the portion of LW that doesn't overlap, we have literary works such as the historical and philosophical texts just mentioned that aren't, at least not primarily, works of art. And in the portion of WA that doesn't overlap, we have works of art that are not verbal, such as painting, sculpture, and architecture. But Gadamer is not so much telling us where to look for truth as he is describing what it is to look for truth beyond scientific method.

So the concept of a work that unites these various domains is not meant to exclude scriptural texts such as the Bible, especially in such culturally crucial translations as the Septuagint, the Vulgate, the King James Version, and the Luther Bible; or political texts such as the Magna Carta, the Declaration of the Rights of Man and Citizen, the Declaration of Independence, and the United States Constitution; or

---

4. David Tracy, *Plurality and Ambiguity: Hermeneutics, Religion, Hope* (San Francisco: Harper & Row, 1987), 12. I shall include the Bible in the category of classic texts not because I do not think it is more than this but because I think it is surely not less.

later works of art, both literary and visual. They are obviously the kind of thing he has in mind. It is just that the humanistic tradition to which he appeals was focused on Greco-Roman antiquity. This particular model is meant to be highly relevant to interpretation and truth in a rich variety of other contexts: legal and theological as well as aesthetic, Eastern as well as Western, popular culture as well as high culture.[5]

Three features of this tradition are especially important to Gadamer. First, although, as we shall see in more detail, he includes non-verbal works of art at the site where truth beyond method is to be found, he has a strong bias toward language. In fact, the entirety of part 3 of *Truth and Method* (roughly the last one hundred pages) is devoted to an analysis of language as the medium of the hermeneutical circle: preunderstanding, interpretation, and new understanding. Language is at once the primary bearer of tradition and itself an ever-changing form of tradition.[6] So it is not surprising to find him saying that it is in the interpretation of works that constitutes the human sciences that "*truth comes to speech*" (*TM* xxiii/xxii).

We might say that when Gadamer speaks of nonverbal works of art he is nevertheless interested in the "language" of art, the way it addresses us and makes a claim on us. He would love Rilke's sonnet, "Archaic Torso of Apollo." For thirteen and a half lines the poem rhapsodizes over this headless stone fragment that "glows." Then it concludes, "You must change your life."[7] Does the poet address these words to himself or to his reader? Surely to himself, even if also to the reader. It is clear that he has been addressed by the work. It has made a claim on him, in this case practical rather than theoretical. It doesn't say "believe this," but rather "live this way," and the poet acknowledges the truth of this claim. He now understands better who he is and who he may become. He has been taught by listening to the language of art. He must aspire to the "noble simplicity and

---

5. Thus my students tell me that their truth, their understanding of how things are, comes far more from their popular culture (music, movies, TV) than from either religion or the high culture of the arts and academic humanities.

6. See note 2 of this chapter.

7. English translation by C. F. MacIntyre, cited by Henry Hatfield in *Aesthetic Paganism in German Literature: From Winckelmann to the Death of Goethe* (Cambridge, MA: Harvard University Press, 1964), 242n65.

tranquil grandeur"[8] found in this partial statue. As Gadamer puts it, the experience of the work of art "does not leave him who has it unchanged" (*TM* 100/86).

Second, a central notion of the humanistic tradition is *Bildung*. This term is often translated as "education," but this is likely to be doubly misleading to us. *Bildung* signifies neither the basic skills of the three R's—readin', ritin', and 'rithmetic—nor the subsequent acquisition of marketable skills so as to be competitive in the job market of an increasingly global economy. A better translation would be "formation" or even "socialization," for it concerns "training in the sensus communis . . . the sense that founds community . . . this communal sense for what is true [theory] and right [practice]" (*TM* 20–21/18–19).[9] The sensus communis "is acquired through living in the community," and in this way "the sense of the community mediates its own positive knowledge" (*TM* 22–23/20–21). This knowledge, of course, is born by practices as well as by propositions, attitudes as well as articulations.

At a very elementary level, *Bildung* and sensus communis are at work when, in response to a child's plaint, "But everybody's doing it," parents respond, "But we aren't everybody else, and in our family that's not what we do." At the level of high culture that is Gadamer's concern (though "low" or popular culture has largely replaced it as the *Bildung* of today's youth),[10] Harold Bloom exhibits the basic idea by treating Shakespeare's works as the Bible of the secular religion to which he belongs.[11] Between these two levels we find the same structures where school children are taught the catechism of American democracy: the Pledge of Allegiance, the Declaration of Independence, and the Bill of Rights.

Finally, to make room for the humanist claim that works of art make truth claims on us, Gadamer calls attention to the difference between this *tradition* and Kant's view of art. Kant separated the

8. The phrase comes from J. J. Winckelmann, the eighteenth-century art historian who helped Germany fall in love with Greek art.

9. See Tracy's definition of a classic work, cited above, as founding community. The term "sensus communis" is not italicized either in the German original or in the translation.

10. What they know by heart are not Bible verses or hymns or a catechism or the Gettysburg address but the lyrics of their favorite popular music.

11. Harold Bloom, *Shakespeare: The Invention of the Human* (New York: Riverhead Books, 1998), xvii–17.

Beautiful (and the Sublime) from the True and the Good. In other words, works of art are not bearers of cognitive significance (theory) or of moral significance (practice). In Gadamer's sense, they do not tell us how things are ("And that's the way it is") or what to do, which is exactly what truth does. What do they do? They provide us with a certain kind of pleasure, a disinterested pleasure that does not seek to own or possess that which pleases. Thus, for example, the pleasure of reading is distinct from the kinds of pleasure we get from eating, drinking, having sex, having status, or owning property. None of these latter pleasures is disinterested.

For Gadamer, such a view is not so much false as it is abstract, or perhaps false simply by being abstract (*TM* 89/77; cf. 85/74). In other words, the point is not to deny that works of art give us a distinctive kind of pleasure. Rather, it is to deny that this is the whole story or even the most fundamental part of the story. The Kantian view abstracts a secondary aspect of the work of art, namely, that it pleases, and completely loses sight of the primary aspect of the work, namely, that it addresses us, that it makes a claim on us that deserves to be called a truth claim. Just as we don't read a text (primarily) to recover the experience of the author but to hear what the author has to say about the subject matter of the text, so we don't turn to the work of art (primarily) for the pleasure we derive but to open ourselves to what it reveals to us about the real.

Incidentally, we may be able to distinguish art from mere entertainment along these lines. In the case of entertainment we read a book, say a mystery novel or spy thriller, or we watch a movie, say a western or a romantic comedy, primarily for the pleasure it gives and not for what we hope to learn about what it means to be human. Of course nothing prohibits a genuine work of art from also being entertaining. If truth is sometimes stranger than fiction, art is also sometimes at least as entertaining as entertainment.

"OK," you say, "but how does the work of art tell us how things are or even how they ought to be? How does it present us with truth beyond method?"

The Truth of the Work of Art

We can begin by speaking of the world of the author and the work. This has a double meaning. On the one hand, it refers to the world in which the author lives and out of which the work emerges, what theologians call the *Sitz im Leben*. As we have seen, the author is an instance of *wirkungsgeschichtliches Bewusstsein*. On the other hand, there is the world created by the author (but not ex nihilo) and presented to us by the work (*TM* 97/83–84). It is what Ricoeur calls the world in front of the text (chap. 5) in contrast to the author's inner life behind the text. In discourse theory it is the *something about something* that someone (author, artist) presents to someone (reader, viewer, listener). It is important to notice that the *something about something* presented by the work of art is not an isolated proposition but a world. Of course it presents only part of a world, but it does so in such a way as to evoke the larger world of which it is a part.

The work presents us with a world. It may be a world of characters and actions; of moods; of faces or fruit; of colors and shapes; of sounds, rhythms, and harmonies; and so forth. In spite of its ties to the world of its origin, this world escapes those horizons and speaks to those of us who inhabit a different world. This is why Tracy could say above that in classic works "there is also the following paradox: though highly particular in origin and expression, classics have the possibility of being universal in their effect." Even if we need notes to understand Shakespeare's locutions, we are addressed, we are moved, and we are changed by reading him. Again with apologies to Walter Cronkite, works of art say to us, "And that's the way it is." Shakespeare's *Othello* and Verdi's *Otello* show us what envy and jealousy are and how close the latter is to real love and yet how far away. In Iago, Othello, and Desdemona, we are shown ourselves, who we are and who we might become.

This is also why Wolterstorff proposes a double hermeneutics with reference to the Bible (chap. 3). We work hard to discover what the human authors of Scripture *said* in the immediate context of the world they shared with their first readers, but we do this not as an end in itself, as if we were uninvolved but curious observers. We want to know what the human authors *said* then in order to hear what the divine author *says* to us here and now. To reduce our reading to that first moment is to proceed abstractly and, by means of a very thin correctness about the past, to protect ourselves from the living truth that would otherwise address us in the present with promises to be trusted and commands to be obeyed.

We need not accede to the claims made on us by the work and the world it presents to us, but if we do we will have learned to see differently, to think differently, to understand differently, and perhaps to live differently. Maurice Merleau-Ponty tells us, "True philosophy consists in relearning to look at the world."[12] Gadamer tells us that classic texts and works of art do the same thing.

The Play

So how do we relearn our way of looking at the world? Speaking of a play, Gadamer writes, "In being presented in play, what is emerges. It produces and brings to light what is otherwise constantly hidden and withdrawn" (*TM* 112/112).[13] In this context, " 'reality' is defined as what is untransformed, and art is the raising up (Aufhebung) of this reality into its truth."[14] Then "everyone recognizes that this is how things are" (*TM* 113/112). No doubt there's a bit of hyperbole in this "everyone." One can ignore the work or resist its claim. But if a work becomes a classic and helps to found and sustain a community, it will be because more than a few people have come to understand themselves and their worlds in its light. The work will be the mediator through which the real is understood. It will play a revelatory role. We may have been envious or jealous or seen envy and jealousy at work in others, but we see more clearly and understand more deeply how things are and how they might be with the help of Shakespeare and Verdi.

If one hears echoes of Plato or Aristotle in the reference to mere reality as "untransformed" and not able to rise up to "its truth," this is no accident. The realm of brute fact, which is probably a figment of our imagination to begin with, is in any case not the realm of meaning and truth. Gadamer lays claim to "the central motif of Platonism" that to know anything is to comprehend the form or idea that is its essence and that makes it what it is. Art calls our attention to the essential structures of the real so that its subject matter

is grasped in its essence, detached from its accidental aspects. . . . This kind of representation leaves behind it everything that is accidental

12. Maurice Merleau-Ponty, *The Phenomenology of Perception*, trans. Colin Smith (London: Routledge and Kegan Paul, 1962), xx.

13. In the background here is Heidegger's notion of truth as disclosedness, uncoveredness, unconcealment, the event of showing and seeing, of revealing and receiving.

14. Perhaps by "untransformed" Gadamer means unnoticed, unrepresented, not understood. See the quotation in the next paragraph.

and unessential. . . . Imitation and representation are not merely a repetition, a copy, but knowledge of the essence. . . . The presentation of the essence, far from being mere imitation, is necessarily revelatory. . . . This is the ground of Aristotle's remark that poetry is more philosophical than history. (*TM* 114–15/113–14)[15]

One important implication of this talk of essence is the diversity that belongs to its unity. For Plato a dog is a dog because it "participates" in or "imitates" the form of dogness, while for Aristotle it is a dog because the form of dogness is actively present in the pooch. (We can leave it to the experts to debate whether this is a substantive or mostly semantic difference.) But it is essential to the essence we awkwardly call dogness that it always manifests itself differently. It is itself by showing itself in different varieties, including the shih tzus and Weimaraners we met in chapter 4. By the same token it is essential to the generic concept of dogness not only that it can actualize itself in a rich variety of species but also that it can actualize itself in an even larger variety of individuals: this Weimaraner, that Weimaraner, and all those other Weimaraners. We are dealing with a complex structure of unity in diversity, oneness in manyness. It is strange in that we don't usually talk about it this way. But it is familiar in that we use it and take it for granted in everyday life, without even noticing— every time, for example, we call this Weimaraner a dog. Just as the Weimaraner shows us (in one way) what it is to be a dog, so a play shows us (in one way) what it is to be human.

The Picture

Gadamer summarizes his analysis of the dramatic work of art and of the performing arts in general (including the nonverbal art of instrumental music) by saying that what appears in the (re)presentation "does not stand like a copy next to the real world, but is that world in the heightened truth of its being. . . . Without being imitated in the work, the world does not exist as it exists in the work. . . . Hence, in presentation, the presence of what is presented reaches its consummation" (*TM* 137/132–33). Then he adds that this

15. Like Gadamer, Plato and Aristotle are philosophers who help us understand how art works.

applies to the plastic or visual arts as well, although they involve
neither language nor performance. The suggestion is that drama and
painting, for example, are like shih tzus and Weimaraners, species
of the same genus.

The picture may approximate a mirror image, as in the case of
a very realistic painting or a photograph. But even then it is not
merely a copy, that is, something present that signifies something
absent. For "the entity itself appears in the image so that we have
the thing itself in the mirror image" (*TM* 138/133). We have here
something analogous to a doctrine of the Real Presence of Christ in
Word or Sacrament. That is why Gadamer applies the same analysis to the religious picture or icon. "Word and image are not mere
imitative illustrations, but allow what they present to be for the
first time fully what it is. . . . The picture is an event of being" (*TM*
143–44/137–38). Since he is speaking about the icon it is not clear
why Gadamer speaks of word as well as of image. Perhaps we can
take it as the suggestion of the real presence of God in all forms of
the Word of God: the incarnate Christ, Scripture, and preaching
based on Scripture. In Colossians 1:15, Christ is described as the
image (εἰκὼν, icon) of the invisible God.

But whether we are talking about a portrait, a still life, a genre
painting, or an icon, "the presentation remains essentially connected
with what is represented—indeed, belongs to it" (*TM* 139/134). Even
the mechanical techniques that in photography give us something
like a mirror image "can be used in an artistic way, when they bring
out something that is not to be found simply by looking. This kind
of picture is not a copy, for it presents something which, without
it, would not present itself in this way." What is pictured "comes to
presentation in the representation. It presents itself there. . . . But
if it presents itself in this way, this is no longer any incidental event
but belongs to its own being. . . . By being presented it experiences,
as it were, an *increase in being*. . . . Essential to an emanation is that
what emanates is an overflow" (*TM* 140/135). Just as the heat and
light that emanate from a fire belong to the fire as part of its essence,
without which it would not be a poor fire but no fire at all, so the
pictorial presentation belongs to the being of what is represented.
Thus, in a bold summary, Gadamer writes that "it is only by being
pictured that a landscape becomes picturesque" (*TM* 142/136). What
is pictured cannot be fully itself apart from the picture. To be is to
be shown, manifested, revealed.

In this formula and throughout his analysis of the picture, Gadamer mixes epistemological and ontological language. On the one hand, he speaks the language of appearing, of (re)presentation, of something presenting itself, of bringing out something. On the other hand, he describes the picture as an event of being and even an increase of being. These two vocabularies are not in conflict. In Gadamer's view it belongs to the very being of things that can be pictured to show or manifest themselves, and for this reason the pictures that help them reveal themselves belong to their very being and bring them toward completion. This event of uncovering, of showing, of manifestation, of revelation is what Gadamer understands by the truth beyond method. Hence the language he uses in making the transition between the play (verbal and performed) and the picture (nonverbal and not performed). "The world that appears in the play of presentation does not stand like a copy next to the real world, but is that world in the heightened truth of its being" (*TM* 137/132). To participate in this event by opening oneself to the work of art is to understand. It is to be nourished by truth. Of course, if our horizons are limited to science and entertainment, calculation and pleasure, we will have trouble understanding what Gadamer is saying. But if we look carefully we are almost bound to find moments where life has taken us beyond such an impoverished world.

Literature

It is obvious that the category of belonging is central to Gadamer's hermeneutics (chaps. 6–7). But it operates at at least three levels, which we need to distinguish with care. First, as *wirkungs-geschichtliches Bewusstsein* we belong to history (tradition) before and throughout our belonging to ourselves. Second, the reader (interpretation) belongs to the text, which does not merely belong to the author, and since the reader always already belongs to history, interpretation will naturally be plural and relative to the historical-linguistic-cultural location of the reader. Third, in the analysis of the work of art we have just been following, the presentation belongs to what is presented just as the heat belongs to the fire, and the world "created" in the work of art belongs to the only world there is, the "real" world, as "the heightened truth of its being," just as the sound belongs to the surf.

This third dimension of belonging serves at least two functions in Gadamer's analysis. Up to now we have focused on the way it helps to answer Gadamer's own question about the nature of truth beyond method. Now we need to see how it points us to that second mode of belonging, the belonging of interpretation to that which is understood. Gadamer's brief discussion of literature (novels, short stories, poems, etc., as distinct from plays) helps us here. It seems that we have two very different kinds of art: performance art (plays and music, for example) and nonperformance art (painting and photography, for example). We might think that literature belongs to this second class, but Gadamer moves to break down the sharp distinction between the two modes. "Reading with understanding is always a kind of reproduction, performance, and interpretation. . . . Like a public reading or performance, being read belongs to literature by its nature" (*TM* 160–61/153–54). A performance is a kind of (public) reading; a reading is a kind of (private) performance. In either case, to perform is to interpret.

Almost immediately after this assimilation of interpretation to performance, Gadamer assimilates it to translation. "The mode of being of a text has something unique and incomparable about it. It presents a specific problem of translation to the understanding" (*TM* 163/156). To perform—either in the narrower sense in which an actor performs a play or a musician performs a sonata or in the broader sense in which to read a novel is to perform it—is to translate. It is to (try to) make it understandable in a semantic context different from that of the author or composer.[16] This is true even for the first "performers," who more nearly than later "performers" belong to the author's world.

We are brought back from the question of truth beyond method to our central theme, interpretation as the mode of access to this truth. These two models of interpretation, as performance and as translation, will deepen Gadamer's answer to Dilthey's and Hirsch's anxiety that the relativity of interpretation means relativism in the sense of an unlimited "anarchy of opinion." Gadamer asks, "Is the meaning of all texts actualized only when they are understood. In

16. Paul Ricoeur tells us that his concept of hermeneutics "comes very near to the concept of translation" (*Debates in Continental Philosophy: Conversations with Contemporary Thinkers*, ed. Richard Kearney [New York: Fordham University Press, 2004], 169). For a sustained analysis of interpretation as translation, see Ricoeur's little gem, *On Translation*, trans. Eileen Brennan (New York: Routledge, 2006).

other words, does being understood belong (gehört) to the meaning of a text just as being heard (Zu-Gehör-Bringen) belongs to the meaning of music? Can we still talk of understanding if we are as free with the meaning of the text as the performing artist with his score?" (*TM* 164/157).

We've noted that you can't beat anybody with nobody. Accordingly, in this chapter we have looked at the notion of truth beyond method that Gadamer places over against the truth that is tied to method. Now we need to do the same with the mode of access that goes with the truth to be found in the work. Gadamer understands this, and over against the Goliath of scientific method he places his David of interpretation as performance and translation. So let us take a closer look at this David.

9

Performance, Application, Conversation

Performance

Gadamer does not deny the usefulness of method and the objectification it involves in both the human sciences and the natural sciences. His claim, along with that of his teacher Heidegger, is rather that interpretation is universal (*TM* xxix–xxx/xxvii). This means that methodical science in any domain is one particular mode of interpretation grounded in its own tradition and possessing its own distinctive strengths and limitations. It is a particular form of *wirkungsgeschichtliches Bewusstsein* and operates within its own hermeneutic circle.[1] It has no special privilege in the domain of the *Geisteswissenschaften* and in fact cuts us off from the mode of truth most distinctive of these disciplines, a truth whose goal is not increased technological control of our environment, natural and social, but increased self-understanding. This is, of course, the kind of truth of primary interest to interpreters of the Bible—academic, pastoral, and lay. When biblical scholars forget that this is their ultimate goal they deprive the living Word

---

1. See the discussion of Helmholtz and Dilthey in chap. 7.

of God of its voice and turn it into "a cadaver handed over for autopsy" (chap. 5).

In exploring this mode of truth, we have seen Gadamer turn to the work in two overlapping modes, the classic text and the work of art. In doing so he first distinguishes the performance arts, such as drama and music, from the nonperformance arts, such as literature; then he breaks down this distinction by suggesting that reading is a kind of performing. The difference is that in the case of the (obviously) performing arts the primary interpreter, the actor who plays Hamlet or the pianist who plays the *Hammerklavier Sonata*, presents an interpretation to the audience, while in the case of the (apparently) nonperforming art the readers (note the plural) of a novel, short story, or poem present an interpretation of the work to themselves.

The Theater and the Concert Hall

Gadamer's general thesis here is that understanding, and thus interpretation, belongs to the very being of the work that is understood by means of interpretation (*TM* xxxi/ xxviii, 164/157). The work is not so much a completed *object* or a thing to be mastered by the methods of some science but rather an *event*, an unfinished event that is brought toward (but not to) completion in the process of interpretation. Tragedies and sonatas are made to be performed. This assimilation of interpretation and performance is more than an analogy because to perform a play or a piece of music is to interpret the script or the score. What Gadamer adds to this is that the structure of performance belongs to all interpretation. All performance is interpretation *and* all interpretation is performance.

This interpretation of interpretation as performances is of enormous importance because it enables Gadamer to give his fullest response to Hirsch's assumption that relativity entails an "anything goes" attitude and to Dilthey's anxiety about the "anarchy of opinion" threatened by hermeneutic pluralism.

There are three things to notice here. First, this pluralism is inherent in the very being of the work. "We ask what this identity is that presents itself so differently in the changing course of ages and circumstances. It does not disintegrate into the changing aspects of itself so that it would lose all identity, but is there in them all.

They all belong to it" (*TM* 120–21/119). We should not be misled by the reference to different ages. Not only do different performers who are historically contemporary give *different* interpretations of the *same* work, but also performers continually tell us that no two performances of their own are the same. The works' "own original essence is always to be something different. . . . An entity that exists only by always being different is temporal in a more radical sense than everything that belongs to history. It has its being only in becoming [difference] and return [identity]" (*TM* 123/121). We understand this structure in terms of the persons we ourselves are. I am the *same* person I was at fifteen and at fifty, but at the same time I am significantly *different*. Barring some psychopathology, there is enough continuity throughout the change and difference to make it unproblematic to say that I (not someone else) am the one who played high school sports at fifteen and had to give up running for walking at fifty because of my knees.

Second, that each performance is a "repetition" of the same thing "does not mean that something is literally repeated. . . . Rather, every repetition is as original as the work itself" (*TM* 122/120). This does not mean that the performer is necessarily as talented as the author or composer. Not even actor Laurence Olivier is on a par with Shakespeare, or pianist Artur Schnabel with Beethoven. But it does mean that each performance is a unique event, just like the composition of the work. It is because every performance is a different interpretation of the same thing and thereby a unique event that interpretation can never be merely reproductive (*TM* 296/296).

Third, this unity in difference is indifferent to the quality of the performance. Thus "however much [the work] is transformed and distorted in being presented, it still remains itself" (*TM* 122/120). I remember hearing Beethoven's violin concerto on the radio years ago. The soloist had become too old to play the first movement at the normal tempo (allegro), so he played it at a dramatically slower pace. It was very different from the Heifetz version, but it was clearly Beethoven's violin concerto and not Bruch's. I would have loved to get a recording of it to play alongside Heifetz. On another occasion I heard an East German pianist playing Chopin, but it was painfully wooden and all too suited to accompany a goose-stepping East German army on parade. I wasn't sure it deserved to be called music, but it was clearly Chopin and not Schubert. It was the same piece, played badly, that I would have loved to hear played well.

Does this ontological indifference to the quality of the performance mean that "anything goes"? Gadamer does not think so and appeals to the very nature of performance against such a conclusion.

> Thus it is not at all a question of mere subjective variety of conceptions, but of the work's own possibilities of being that emerge as the work explicates itself, as it were, in the variety of its aspects [like our friend the elephant]. . . . But one fails to appreciate the obligatoriness of the work of art [or classic text] if one regards the variations possible in the presentation as free and arbitrary. In fact they are all subject to the supreme criterion of "right" representation. (*TM* 118/117)

Because the presentation is "bound" to the work, the former cannot be "arbitrary" but must be "correct" (*TM* 119/118). In other words, if I am playing Hamlet I am not free to say "To fish or not to fish" instead of "To be or not to be." Nor am I free to play an A-flat every time the score of the *Hammerklavier Sonata* calls for a C-sharp. Because of these constraints, Gadamer speaks of presentations as "obligatory" and "bound" rather than "arbitrary" and as needing to be "right" or "correct."
However:

> the fact that the representation is bound to the work is not lessened by the fact that this bond can have no fixed criterion . . . and yet we would regard the canonization of a particular interpretation . . . as a failure to appreciate the real task of interpretation . . . which imposes itself on every interpreter immediately, in its own way, and does not allow him to make things easy for himself by simply imitating a model. . . . In view of the finitude of our historical existence, it would seem that there is something absurd about the whole idea of a unique, correct interpretation. (*TM* 119–20/118)

One sometimes reads in the advertising for a music CD that it is the "definitive" interpretation of a given work, but music lovers know that there is no such thing and that this is commercial hyperbole for the claim that this is an outstanding performance. Doesn't hyperbole pass into arrogance whenever we present "our" theology as the definitive interpretation of the Bible?

It would seem, then, that we have three classes of performance. First, there are those that simply get it wrong, that in this or that respect are incorrect. The script or the score has been violated. Nothing Gadamer says eliminates this possibility. Second, there are those interpretations that get it right—play all the right notes in all the right rhythms, as with our East German pianist, or say all the right words in the right order—but in such a poor way that we call the interpretation right but regrettable. Finally, there are those interpretations that get it right and that are judged by the most knowledgeable and discriminating judges (the critics) to be good, even superb, world-class performances.

The important point here is obvious. There will be a plurality of performances that will fall into this third category, each *different* from the others although they are presentations of the *same* work. In this way "the work's own possibilities of being . . . emerge . . . in the variety of its aspects" (*TM* 118/117). Here we see concretely what Gadamer means when he says that "understanding is not merely a reproductive but always a productive activity as well" (*TM* 296/296). If the interpretation is not to be arbitrarily subjective, it will have to submit to the constraint of the script, the score, the text. This is the reproductive moment, what Derrida calls "doubling commentary" (chap. 5). But this reproductive activity, as Derrida puts it, can serve as a "guardrail" only because it is the necessary but not sufficient condition of a good interpretation (chap. 5, note 12). Because interpretation is always also productive, there will be a variety of "correct" interpretations that differ from one another, for example, Olivier's Hamlet and Kenneth Branagh's, Heifetz's Beethoven and Anne-Sophie Mutter's. They will be judged by "flexible" criteria (*TM* 119/118) of faithfulness and illuminating power that go beyond mechanical reproduction. If mechanical reproduction were sufficient, the photos I take would be on a par with those of Ansel Adams, but no one, including myself, thinks they are; the truth claims of the work will be what they illuminate and are faithful to.

A Similar Model: Translation

Gadamer finds the same structure of limited and nonarbitrary relativity and plurality in another domain: translation.[2]

---

2. At *TM* 163/156 Gadamer treats "deciphering" and "interpretation" as interchangeable, but not in the sense given above (chaps. 5 and 6), where deciphering is merely reproductive.

The translator [performer, reader] must translate the meaning to be understood into the context in which the other speaker lives. This does not, of course, mean that he is at liberty to falsify the meaning of what the other person [author] says. Rather, the meaning must be preserved, but since it must be understood within a new language world, it must establish its validity in a new way. Thus every translation is at the same time an interpretation. (*TM* 384/386)

There are constraints on the translator, whose work is "bound" to the text and must be "correct." The translator is not free to translate an aorist tense verb in the future tense or to render *Ich liebe dich* or *Je t'aime* as "I dislike anchovies." Once again, we have three kinds of translations. There will be those that don't get it right, that are bad translations because of the mistakes translators make. There will be those that get it right but are wooden or archaic or fail in some other way to convey the meaning skillfully from one world to another. Then there will be those that get it right and are faithful to the meaning of the text by effectively conveying it from one world to another. Thus in translating the Bible into Sioux, a good translation will probably render references to the kings of Israel and to God as King of kings with the Siouan word for chief.

This last group will be the good translations, even the superb ones, *and* once again there will be a diverse plurality of them. Just as there are no "definitive" performances of a play or a sonata, so there is no "definitive" translation of a classic text. I can, of course, have a favorite Hamlet or *Hammerklavier* or translation of the Bible. But I would be foolish to claim that one is right and all the others are wrong, and I would be wise to consult a variety of the "best" translations if I want to understand, for example, a particular biblical passage (even if I can read it in the original language). Here again hermeneutic pluralism is not anarchy but a combination of discipline and freedom employed more or less successfully in the service of the text and ultimately of its subject matter.

The implications for biblical interpretation are clear. If, as Gadamer argues, every translation is an interpretation and, conversely, every interpretation is a translation, that is, carrying meaning over from one context to another, then every theology is a translation. Accordingly, it would be foolish to claim that there is one "definitive" theology that is right while all the others are wrong (though theologies, like other interpretations/translations, can be wrong).

Rather, it would be wise to consult a variety of the "best" theologies if we want to understand the Bible and ultimately its subject matter: God and our relation to God.

Application

We must look more closely at what it means for a translator to convey a meaning from one world (linguistic, cultural, social) to another. When two persons engage in conversation, two different worlds come into contact. Even if the two are identical twins living at the same time and raised in the same family, they inhabit (or are) two different, though possibly very similar, worlds (networks of meaning and truth, horizons). When we say that they have understood each other, we do not mean that they have become identical so that the difference between them has been obliterated and there is now only one person or point of view. What we mean is that the two worlds, which we can think of as circles, are no longer eccentric to each other or merely tangential but that they have overlapped sufficiently that we somehow feel warranted in saying that they understand rather than that they misunderstand each other. This need not mean that they agree about the truth of the matter under discussion, only that they understand the truth claims inherent in each other's discourse.

It is, at any rate, along these lines that Gadamer distinguishes understanding, the goal of interpretation, from misunderstanding. He calls it the "fusion of horizons" (*TM* 301–7/301–6). Visually, and by extension linguistically and conceptually, a horizon is the ever-moving circle whose center I am, within which I can see whatever I can (at the moment) "see" and beyond which whatever remains (for the moment) is "invisible."

In speaking about the fusion of horizons, Gadamer does indeed speak of "one great horizon" and "a single historical horizon" (*TM* 304/303). But this does not mean that the horizonal-historical distance between author and reader is obliterated (*TM* 297/297). It "always involves rising to a higher universality that overcomes not only our own particularity but also that of the other" (*TM* 305/304). Successful translation means that the two worlds do not remain merely particular—alien, closed, eccentric to each other—but become part of a larger community within which differences are not abolished but mediated by conversation that effects understanding.

We need only to imagine here the difference between an occupying army that does not speak the local language and that same army accompanied by a translator who does. In the latter case understanding can be achieved, even if agreement is not. Or we might think of a marriage counselor who (1) asks, say, the wife to tell how she sees the situation; (2) then asks the husband to tell not how he sees the situation but how his wife sees it; and (3) then asks the wife whether her husband has heard her, has understood her discourse. It is easy to imagine it might take more than one try to get to the place where she feels that she has been understood and the process can be repeated in the opposite direction. Here again, understanding does not presuppose agreement but an adequate grasp of the truth claims borne by the speech acts.

Although we are speaking about texts, these examples from ordinary conversation are appropriate. Gadamer regularly insists that texts speak to us, address us, make claims on us. They are not objects to be seen but voices to be heard. The question is not merely "What did this text once mean to its author and the original readers?" but always *also* "What does it mean for me or for us here and now?" In other words, for Gadamer application to the present is an integral part of interpretation. His triad is understanding, interpretation, and application. The three together comprise "one unified process. . . . We consider application to be just as integral a part of the hermeneutical process as are understanding and interpretation" (*TM* 308/306–7).

We have already considered the first two. Within the hermeneutical circle we interpret on the basis of a preunderstanding (pre-judice), which may be revised or replaced, leading to new interpretations. But we short-circuit the process if we fail to see that "understanding always involves something like applying the text to be understood to the interpreter's present situation" (*TM* 307–8/306–7). Interpretation must be faithful to both the past and the present if it is to bring meaning from the latter to the former (*TM* 310/309; 326–27/322–23). A text has a single past, though it may be a very complex confluence of components. But it has many subsequent presents into which many interpreters will seek to translate its meaning. So there will be a diversity of readers who present (perform, translate) this *same* meaning to themselves or to others *differently* insofar as their interpretations are relative to a variety of *different* contexts. Application is especially important for Christians interpreting the Bible because their "vocation is to *embody* Scripture. . . . Unless Christian communities are committed to embodying their Scriptural interpretation, the Bible loses its character as Scripture."[3]

Two features of application are especially important to Gadamer. One is that application concerns practice and not just theory. For this reason he assimilates interpretation to what Aristotle calls practical wisdom (*phronesis*) rather than theoretical wisdom (*nous, episteme, sophia*).[4] The texts that concern Gadamer do not merely give rise to theories of various sorts; they found and nourish communities in their life together, partly by describing how things are but especially by prescribing how they can and should be.

This emphasis on the practical, behavioral nature of application should come as no surprise. In the context of discourse theory (chap. 3) we saw that speech acts are not limited to assertions of fact. There are imperatives as well as indicatives, calls to actions and attitudes of a particular kind. Wolterstorff pointed out that typical divine speech acts are promises and commands rather than mere assertions of what is the case. We have also seen Rilke find an imperative in a headless statue of Apollo (chap. 8): "You must change your life."

I am reminded of a pamphlet I read long ago in which Luther suggested four questions we should bring with us every time we read the Bible or hear it read: What am I to believe? What am I to do? Of what am I to repent? For what am I to give thanks? In a Lutheran context, even the first question takes us beyond the purely theoretical or factual domain to the personal and practical realms, for, above all, the promises of God as they apply to us here and now are to be believed on hearing the Word of God. Here, to believe is to trust and to act on that trust. An earlier version of this kind of thinking tells us that, inspired by God, Scripture is "useful for teaching, for reproof, for correction, and for training in righteousness" (2 Tim. 3:16).

Second, application involves making the meaning concrete, that is, giving specific and detailed meaning to abstract language (*TM*

---

3. Stephen E. Fowl and L. Gregory Jones, *Reading in Communion: Scripture and Ethics in Christian Life* (Grand Rapids: Eerdmans, 1991), 1, 20. This embodiment can also be described as *performing* Scripture. See ibid., 62–64, 80.

4. Without mentioning either Aristotle or Gadamer, Fowl and Jones affirm that interpretation requires "the virtue of practical wisdom" (*Reading in Communion*, 30, 39). It is not just a matter of skills but of skills and virtues, that is, habits of character (ibid., 35–36, 40, 49).

329/325). Take, for example, the words "all men are created equal" in the Declaration of Independence. It has a nice ring, but to understand it is to give it concrete meaning in various acts of interpretation that apply it to specific contexts. In the Constitution as originally written, "men" was not a gender-free reference to all humans, for slaves of either gender and women were not included. Women were not given the right to vote until the Nineteenth Amendment (1920), and the status of slaves as property was left unchallenged, though they were to be counted as three-fifths of a person when determining how many members each state could send to the House of Representatives. The Emancipation Proclamation, the Fourteenth Amendment, and subsequent civil rights legislation, such as the Civil Rights Act of 1964 and the Voting Rights Act of 1965, have interpreted and understood Jefferson's words in the act of applying them, making them concrete in ways dramatically different from their original application and thus from their original meaning.

Gadamer expresses the inseparability of understanding and interpretation and application by saying, with reference to Aristotle's conception of practical wisdom, that for Aristotle

> application did not consist in relating some pregiven universal to the particular situation. The interpreter dealing with a traditionary text tries to apply it to himself. But this does not mean that the text is given for him as something universal, that he first understands it per se, and then afterward uses it for particular applications. . . . He must relate the text to this situation if he wants to understand at all. (*TM* 324/321)

Thus, for example, I do not understand what "Thou shalt not kill" means unless I know whether it permits killing in war, capital punishment, or lethal self-defense, and if allowed in any of these cases, under what circumstances. Similarly, I do not understand what "cruel and unusual punishment" or "torture" is apart from applications that specify which acts are precluded and which are permitted and to what degree. To understand is to apply; to apply differently is to understand differently.

There is a marked difference here from Hirsch. Hirsch wants to separate sharply what he calls meaning from what he calls significance. "*Meaning* is that which is represented by a text; it is what the author meant by his use of a particular sign sequence; it is what the signs represent. *Significance*, on the other hand, names a relationship between that meaning and a person, or a conception, or a situation, or indeed anything imaginable." Or, to put this last point more succinctly, significance is a meaning's "value or its present relevance" (*VI* 8, 57).[5]

We have already seen why Hirsch wants to make this distinction as sharp as possible (chap. 4). He believes that (1) what the author meant is a single, determinate, unchangeable meaning; (2) the author's meaning can be objectively identified; (3) the significance of this fixed, determinate meaning will be as diverse as the contexts into which it finds its way; and (4) the relativity of significance to numerous, different contexts will result in an "anything goes" relativism if it is not rigorously excluded from the task of interpretation. So he insists that significance is not "the proper object . . . of interpretation, whose exclusive object is verbal meaning" (*VI* 57).[6]

It is clear that "significance" and "application" are roughly synonymous. Both are concerned with what the text has to say to us here and now, and, consequently, both involve diversity and relativity in understanding a text. Gadamer's quarrel with Hirsch concerns the second and the fourth of the theses of the previous paragraph. Regarding (2), he is less sanguine than Hirsch that we can be fully objective in the linguistic-psychological or grammatical-historical task of identifying the author's understanding of his or her own text. This is partly because of doubts about the full transparency of authorial self-consciousness to itself and partly because the research involved takes place within a hermeneutical circle that is not free of presuppositions. Still, by speaking of a *reproductive* dimension to interpretation, he would seem to acknowledge that this task, which he sees as preliminary, should aim at the highest degree of objectivity possible. After all, its goal is to reproduce authorial meaning that, as our Jefferson example suggests, includes authorial application.

5. We could describe this two-step procedure as "excavate" and then "apply," where the first presupposes a disinterested, disengaged spectator and the second the opposite. See Fowl and Jones, *Reading in Communion*, 4. Like Gadamer, whom they do not mention, they oppose this separation. See also *VI* 57–58.

6. By "verbal meaning" is to be understood the author's verbal meaning, what the author meant. To say that "all men are created equal" means that women and African Americans should have a right to vote equal to that of white males is surely also to express a verbal meaning. The different application gives a different verbal meaning.

But while Gadamer grants that the reproductive aspect of interpretation can be distinguished from the productive, past meaning from present meaning, he rejects the notion that they can be separated. By designating water as H_2O we distinguish the hydrogen from the oxygen. But if we were to separate the two, we would no longer have water. So the heart of Gadamer's difference from Hirsch concerns (4). Once again there are two reasons not to separate interpretation from application or significance.

First, while Gadamer agrees that significance or application will be pluralistic and relative to the contexts in which interpretation occurs, he denies, as we have just seen, that this relativity entails an "anything goes" attitude. There are constraints on the whole process, which must be faithful to the past as well as to the present. The simple either/or between the one and only right interpretation, which merely duplicates authorial meaning, and the chaotic anarchy feared by Hirsch and Dilthey is arbitrary and abstract. People don't take *Ich liebe dich* or *Je t'aime* to mean "I don't like anchovies, and therefore I should eat them as a Lenten penance," and if they did we would have no problem with telling them they are badly mistaken.

Second, Gadamer's view is that authorial meaning, the reproductive moment, is preliminary and not primary. In reading texts that remain part of a living canon, we are not curious, antiquarian spectators at a museum (or mausoleum) whose fundamental question is "What language game did they play once upon a time?" That is an important but penultimate part of the attempt to hear what the texts have to say to us here and now. So it just isn't the case that authorial meaning is "the proper object" of interpretation. It is *a proper but penultimate object* in the service of *the proper object*, namely, what the text has to say to us here and now. The goal of biblical interpretation is holy living.

In spite of his own anxieties about relativism, Wolterstorff is closer to Gadamer than to Hirsch on this point. His theological double hermeneutics makes the question, "What did the biblical writer say back then?" preliminary to the primary question, "What is God saying to us here and now through what the biblical writer said?" (chap. 3). For him as for Gadamer, to reduce the hermeneutical task to a question about the past is to think abstractly, to confuse an essential part of the process for the whole.

Gadamer tries to support this latter claim by looking at the three fields of interpretation that Schleiermacher tried to unite in a general—or as Ricoeur puts it, "deregionalized"—hermeneutics (chap. 2): literature (or "philology"), law, and theology. Gadamer thinks the inseparability of interpretation from application is most obvious in the latter two cases.

> In both legal and theological hermeneutics there is an essential tension between the fixed text—the law [Constitution or statute] or the gospel—on the one hand and, on the other, the sense arrived at by applying it at the concrete moment of interpretation, either in judgment or in preaching. A law does not exist in order to be understood historically, but to be concretized in its legal validity by being interpreted. Similarly, the gospel does not exist in order to be understood as a merely historical document, but to be taken in such a way that it exercises its saving effect. This implies that the text, whether law or gospel, if it is to be understood properly—i.e., according to the claim it makes—must be understood at every moment, in every concrete situation, in a new and different way. Understanding here is always application. (*TM* 308–9/307–8)

In these contexts, "To distinguish between a normative function [the claim addressed to us now] and a cognitive one [the meaning as understood by the author(s)] is to separate what clearly belong together."[7] Moreover, "The meaning of a law that emerges in its normative application is fundamentally no different from the meaning reached in understanding a text" (*TM* 311/309). In other words, legal interpretation is a model for all interpretation of texts that are more than dead artifacts.

The point is perhaps not so obvious in the case of philology,[8] which for Gadamer now includes philosophical as well as literary texts (*TM* 332–33/328). Because the interpretation of such texts is interested in both their beauty and their truth, that is, their "exemplary" character (*TM* 335/331; 337–38/332–33), in interpreting them "we do not have the freedom to adopt a historical distance toward

---

7. I have argued that we can distinguish the two conceptually without thinking that they can be separated in fact or that the latter dimension is primary. I think Gadamer would agree to this more careful formulation.

8. But Gadamer would say "Amen" to Alasdair MacIntyre's suggestion that "the heroic literature provided a central part of the moral scriptures of those later societies" that still took them seriously (MacIntyre, *After Virtue: A Study in Moral Theory* [Notre Dame, IN: University of Notre Dame Press, 1981], 123). Recall Bloom's account of Shakespeare as the Bible of his secular religion (chap. 8).

them" since what makes historical research scientific "is precisely
the fact that it objectifies tradition and methodically eliminates the
influence of the interpreter and his time on understanding" (*TM*
333/328–29). According to the self-understanding of history as objectively scientific, it is "fundamentally impossible for [the historian]
to regard himself as the addressee of the text and accept its claim
on him" precisely because, unlike the judge and the preacher, he is
only "trying to discover something about the past through them. . . .
He has given up the claim that his texts have a normative validity
for him" (*TM* 335/330–31; 337/332).

We are obviously speaking here of what Gadamer calls the reproductive dimension of hermeneutics (chap. 5). It is quite possible
for the practitioners of philology (philosophy and literature, not to
mention theology) to think of themselves in terms of this model of
the historian. All three would be asking only one question: What
language games did they play back then?

Gadamer's response is twofold. On the one hand, if we accept
this account of historical research, then philosophy and literary
criticism can retain their humanistic mission only by resisting the
temptation to claim scientific objectivity for their work. More important, Gadamer asks

> whether the picture of the historical approach, as set out here, is
> not itself distorted. Perhaps not only the approach of the critic and
> philologist but *also that of the historian* should be oriented not so
> much to the methodological ideal of the natural sciences as to the
> model offered us by legal and theological hermeneutics. . . . What
> makes the historian is understanding the significance [note Hirsch's
> term] of what he finds. (*TM* 338/334)

To be sure, the historian wants to establish the facts. "But the
facts are not the real objects of inquiry; they are simply material for
the real tasks of . . . the historian—that is . . . to reach a just deci-
sion and to establish the historical significance of an event within
the totality of his historical self-consciousness" (*TM* 338/334). In
other words, even for the historian as well as the reader of philosophical, literary, legal, and scriptural texts, "all reading involves
application, so that a person reading a text is himself part of the
meaning he apprehends. He belongs to the text he is reading" (*TM*
340/335).

Conversation

Gadamer repeatedly stresses that classic texts speak to us, address us, make claims on us about what is right and good and true. In this respect they are more like persons with whom we engage in conversation than objects we subject to some methodical observation. So we have one more model of interpretation. It is like (1) performing a play or sonata; (2) translating from one language into another; (3) applying the law to a particular, concrete situation; (4) applying a scriptural text to the life of believers; and now (5) carrying on a conversation. The goal in every case is understanding. The means in no case is an objectifying method, one that turns the subject matter into an object to be observed and the observer into a disinterested, "objective" spectator, free from presuppositions and perspectives. There are constraints but there are no fixed rules in the sense of being beyond discussion and debate.

There are four important features to Gadamer's notion of interpretation as conversation. First, it requires an openness, even a vulnerability, to the voice of another. This means genuine listening. "Openness to the other, then, involves recognizing that I myself must accept some things that are against me, even though no one else forces me to do so" (*TM* 361/355). The presupposition here is that I am aware of my "finitude and limitedness" and realize that I might learn something. I have "the knowledge of not knowing. This is the famous Socratic docta ignorantia [learned ignorance]" (*TM* 362/356).

The Socratic dialogues are Gadamer's model here, and at least in his interpretation their most important feature is not the deconstructive, refutational aspect but the wisdom that knows its own ignorance—the very opposite of the know-it-all. Just for that reason the negative aspect just mentioned is directed against opinion, not as an inferior mode of knowledge to be replaced by a superior philosophical intuition,[9] but as an almost psychoanalytic resistance to openness. "Opinion has a curious tendency to propagate itself. . . . How, then, can ignorance be admitted and questions arise? . . . A person skilled in the 'art' of questioning is a person who can prevent questions from being suppressed by the dominant opinion" (*TM* 366–67/359–61).

9. When he moves in this direction, Plato parts company with Socrates.

Second, these references to questions and questioning are essential and not accidental. The conversation Gadamer has in mind consists in reciprocal questioning. The text, by making truth claims on us, puts us in question. Have you taken this into account? Have you seen this aspect of the matter? Have you noticed the implications for how you live your life? And so forth.

We might think that the appropriate response to a question is an answer. But Gadamer suggests that the appropriate response is to ask one's own questions. Those in the Socratic dialogues who were quick to give answers to Socrates's questions were the embodiment of what has just been called "opinion," and which might also have been called dogmatism or fundamentalism. They had no need to learn and, therefore, to listen; they already had all the answers. They live in a world of myth, defined somewhere by Camus as the world of all answers and no questions. Moreover, what is needed is not just the willingness to question and to be questioned but also the ability to do so, which is not automatic. As every scientist knows, learning how to ask good questions is at least as important and as difficult as learning how to test various answers.

Third, when conversation takes place willingly and humbly, the partners "are far less the leaders of it than the led. . . . All this shows that a conversation has a spirit of its own" (TM 383/385). We express this idea when we talk of following the argument or the evidence wherever it may lead. Since the assumption is (1) that the parties acknowledge that they don't already know all they need to know and (2) that they are not so wedded to the current "opinion" that they practice what Charles Sanders Peirce calls "the method of tenacity"[10] to cling to it, the parties will sometimes be surprised to discover where the conversation leads. While this is rather easy to understand when the conversation is between two persons, it is a bit puzzling when one of the partners is a text, especially if that text is the Bible. But perhaps we could say, with a bit of imagination, that the Bible was surprised to learn, say, that its proclamation of the gospel called for the abolition of slavery.

This leads to the fourth and final characteristic of a Gadamerian conversation: the goal is not to win by making one's own original

10. Charles Sanders Peirce, "The Fixation of Belief," in *Collected Papers of Charles Sanders Peirce*, vol. 5, *Pragmatism and Pragmaticism*, ed. Charles Hartshorne and Paul Weiss (Cambridge, MA: Harvard University Press, 1960), 233–36.

viewpoint prevail. "To reach an understanding in a dialogue is not merely a matter of putting oneself forward and successfully asserting one's own point of view, but being transformed into a communion in which we do not remain what we were" (*TM* 379/371).

Most of Gadamer's talk about interpretation as conversation is put in terms of "entering into dialogue with the text." But he insists that the model of a conversation between persons in spoken language is "more than a metaphor" (*TM* 368/361–62). One reason is that the two "conversations" have the same goal, namely, coming to understand the truth claims that are addressed to one by a voice other than one's own.

But there is another reason that is at least equally important even if not explicitly developed in keeping with its importance. If the conversation between and among persons points to and illuminates the conversation between reader and text, the reverse is also true. The dialogue with the text implicates a dialogue among readers.

How so? As a reader my dialogue with the text takes place within the hermeneutical circle. As I am open to the text, listen to it carefully, and let it lead me to ideas that may well be "against me," I revise or replace my operative presuppositions. But how do I know whether my changes represent progress? Politicians call any change they support "reform." But the honorific term is not automatically merited. Similarly, the changes in my horizon that reading and listening, questioning and being questioned lead to may or may not represent a deepened understanding of the subject matter. How can I tell? Within what Ricoeur calls the "conflict of interpretations," how do I distinguish the better ones from the worse ones. Perhaps I've just exchanged my narrow view of the elephant as a kind of rope for an equally narrow view of the elephant as a kind of tree trunk (chap. 1).

Gadamer's conversation model implies a clear answer. As part of my conversation with the text I need to carry on a conversation with other interpreters. Although blind (Socratic ignorance), the six men from Hindustan, with a narrowly perspectival and therefore a seriously distorted idea of an elephant, might have come to a less inadequate view if they had shared their insights with one another and in the process broadened their horizons. It is this movement from a particular perspective to a more universal point of view that is the goal of *Bildung* (chap. 8). It is the fusion of horizons.

Classic texts found communities, are sustained by communities, and in turn sustain communities. But this means that their interpretation is also a communal affair, a dialogical and not a monological process. It takes place among individuals within a community and among communities. If the Bible is the "classic text" of the Christian church, that church, in turn, is the community of the Bible's interpretation. It belongs to the church's identity that it is the conversation in which its members and its communities seek to understand the Bible and its subject matter: God and our relation to God.

10

Conversation and the Liberal-Communitarian Debate

Political Liberalism: A Model for the Church?

By Christian hermeneutics let us understand the theory and especially the practice of interpreting the Bible as "performed" in three modes: written, spoken, and silent. Although all who interpret the Bible can rightly be called theologians, we can stick closer to ordinary usage and distinguish theologians, whose interpretations are written in books and articles, from pastors, whose interpretations are primarily oral in the form of sermons, and from lay persons, whose interpretations take place in the silence of devotional reading.[1] Of course, when lay persons function as Sunday school teachers, catechists, or parents, they fill a role like that of the preacher, passing on their interpretations orally to others.

We have just seen that a major implication of Gadamerian hermeneutics is that this task is doubly conversational. It is a con-

---

1. We can also include the interpretation of the works of those Christian writers who form the theological, as distinct from the biblical, canon: the Cappadocians, Augustine, Anselm, Aquinas, Luther, Calvin, Wesley, and so forth.

versation between reader and text to be "translated," "performed," "embodied," and it is a conversation among readers (and traditions of reading). This means that the church *is,* among other things, a communal conversation seeking to understand more deeply its founding, "classic" text, the Bible, and the traditions of interpretation that have developed through the centuries.[2]

The nature of these conversations will be illuminated by Gadamer's "deregionalized," general hermeneutics that *describes* what actually happens when individuals and communities interpret classic texts (Shakespeare, the Constitution, the Bible). But some *normative* considerations may well emerge by returning to special hermeneutics, in our case theological hermeneutics. A proper understanding of what kind of community the church is may well provide guidelines for the conversation.

At this point we could turn immediately to ecclesiology, that branch of systematic theology that concerns the nature and mission of the church. But since we've already been exploring some philosophical conversations in the hope of gaining insight for our theological tasks, let us linger a bit longer to see if Athens can be helpful to Jerusalem.

At least since the publication of *After Virtue* by Alasdair MacIntyre in 1981,[3] there has been a "liberal/communitarian" debate among philosophers.[4] The two sides are often at cross-purposes since, we shall see, they are not offering conflicting answers to the same question. Because our interests are theological, no attempt will be made to treat these traditions comprehensively. Only certain features will be considered and only as heuristic devices for thinking about the church as a communal conversation of interpretation.

Let us first look at political liberalism. It is a conceptual ellipse whose two foci are the notions of individual rights and limited government. The rights of individuals are considered to be natural rights,

2. That the hermeneutical task involves both Scripture and tradition (see the previous note) will be true, de facto, regardless of our theological view about the relation of the two and regardless of the degree to which we are aware of and willing to acknowledge the role of tradition in guiding our interpretations of both Scripture and subsequent traditions.

3. Alasdair MacIntyre, *After Virtue: A Study in Moral Theory* (Notre Dame, IN: University of Notre Dame Press, 1981).

4. Michael Sandel, ed., *Liberalism and Its Critics* (New York: New York University Press, 1984), draws on earlier writings by various authors in staging this debate.

at least in the sense that their warrant precedes the laws of the land. Examples would include the God-given, unalienable rights stated in the Declaration of Independence (1776) along with those specified in the Bill of Rights (1791), the French Declaration of the Rights of Man and of the Citizen (1789), and the United Nations' Universal Declaration of Human Rights (1948). The notion of limited government is twofold in relation to these rights: government's primary task, sometimes its only task, is to protect its citizens as possessors of these rights from those who would violate them, and must never itself violate these rights either by law or outside the law.

Political liberalism owes its birth largely to two historical processes. One parent is the long struggle to limit the power of the monarch and eventually, in the case of the American Revolution, of government even in its parliamentary form.[5] Even in democracy, the minorities need to be protected from the majority. The Magna Carta (1215) signifies symbolically, if not in actual fact, the beginning of this process. The other parent is the long struggle for religious liberty and freedom of conscience in the aftermath of the Reformation. It shattered the facade of Europe as a united and coherent Christendom. In its aftermath, wars of religion and various forms of religious intolerance and persecution made religion a major partner with dynastic ambition in the perpetration of violence, suffering, and oppression.[6] Creedal anathemas were not mere religious rhetoric but all too often became deadly declarations of war.

The solution that emerged was the secularization of government in varying degrees, the creation of a nonsectarian political space in which the coercive power of government would neither privilege nor persecute citizens on the basis of their religion. In the United States this came to be known as the separation of church and state. Accordingly, the First Amendment in the Bill of Rights specifies a series of political rights—freedom of speech and of the press along with the rights to assemble and to petition the government for redress of grievances—but only after first requiring that "Congress shall make no law respecting an establishment of religion, or prohibiting the free exercise thereof."

5. The Stamp Act of 1765 was an act of Parliament, not a royal edict.
6. See Roland Bainton, *The Travail of Religious Liberty: Nine Biographical Studies* (Philadelphia: Westminster, 1951).

It is important to be clear at the outset that *liberal* in this context is not about the difference between Democrats and Republicans, left-wing and right-wing policy preferences. The basic framework of what is sometimes called rights-liberalism or classical liberalism includes a spectrum that runs from left to right (or right to left). Toward the left end of the spectrum one finds a democratic socialism or welfare-state liberalism that rests on a more expansive understanding of the rights to be protected by government and a sense that government can protect its citizens only by actively promoting them but never violating them. Toward the right end of the spectrum one finds a "that government governs best that governs least"[7] conservatism or libertarianism that rests on a more restrictive understanding of rights and sees the government's task only to protect and not to promote them. Thus the notion of the minimal, "night watchman state."[8] In this respect, liberalism might well be a model for a church that includes a spectrum from left to right (or right to left) theologically.

Political liberalism articulates a mode of life together in a given *state*. Is it a helpful model in any sense for the *church*? Well, no. And maybe. The rights it seeks to protect both by and from government power are in the first instance rights of individuals, and rights-liberalism is regularly described as an individualistic political philosophy. Ontologically this seems to imply that I am a fully human person prior to being a citizen; citizenship is accidental and external to my identity, not essential and internal. Sociologically the implication seems to be that the state to which I belong is only a means to my individual ends.

An economist friend of mine once expressed this idea very eloquently (without realizing it). He saw the government as something similar to his insurance company. If he got good services for a reasonable price, it was a good arrangement. His identity was in no way involved. Just as up to the age of eighteen he was not a participating (voting) citizen, so also until he owned his own car he was not a customer of any insurance company, but he was fully himself. That becoming a customer was accidental and external to his identity was

7. This saying has been attributed to Thomas Jefferson and Thomas Paine, among others, but it is probably an anonymous proverb that antedates all of them.

8. As developed in Robert Nozick, *Anarchy, State, and Utopia* (New York: Basic Books, 1974).

clear from the fact that changing from Allstate to State Farm or GEICO would not in any significant sense make him a different person.

My relationship to my insurance company is contractual, and the idea of the state as the product of a social contract is closely related to political liberalism.[9] While the insurance contract is between me and my company, the Lockean social contract is among the citizens (to be) and is an agreement among themselves to set up a government for their protection in light of the "inconveniences" of the state of nature.[10] In either case, the basis for the relationship is not that of shared values but of mutual advantage, and I naturally view my company or my country as a means to my own private ends.

Just for the record, liberalism need not be so understood. It can be about the shared values that give us our collective identity. For left-leaning liberals like John Rawls and Ronald Dworkin, liberalism is the answer to the question, "How can *we* be a *just* and *fair* society?" For right-leaning liberals like Friedrich Hayek and Robert Nozick, liberalism is the answer to the question, "How can *we* be a *free* people?"[11] It's not about how I can get the most for my money but about our most basic shared values as a *political* society. This can be seen clearly enough in the Preamble to the United States Constitution:

> We the People of the United States, in Order to form a more perfect Union, establish Justice, insure domestic Tranquility, provide for the common defense, promote the general Welfare, and secure the Blessings of Liberty to ourselves and our Posterity, do ordain and establish this Constitution for the United States of America.

However, in a consumerist, litigious society with an entitlement ethos, it is not hard (or rare) to think of government in individualist, instrumental terms.

9. This is especially true in its Lockean form as developed in *Two Treatises of Government* (1690). The foundation of the state is developed in the second of these treatises after the first, significantly, develops an all-out assault on the "divine right of kings" theory.

10. In *The Political Theory of Possessive Individualism: Hobbes to Locke* (Oxford: Clarendon, 1962), C. B. Macpherson points out that the "state of nature" is not the pretribal hunting-and-gathering family we might suspect but includes all the basic elements of a capitalist economy.

11. These four are representatives of rights-liberalism in Sandel, *Liberalism and Its Critics*.

How well does such a model fit the church? That it is easy to think of the church along these lines is clear from the following prayer, which I clipped from somewhere years ago:

Please Pastor—Help Me

Life is hard. I hurt.
I cannot find relief.
I cannot find comfort . . .

I am under this burden every day. . . . Be merciful, be comforting. . . . Let your people know the treasures to be found in Jesus Christ so they can help me too. Please do not let me return to this cold, hard life without help.

Here the church, like the family, is perceived as a "haven in a heartless world."[12] I go to church, as I might go to group therapy, to get help in dealing with my personal needs and problems.

There is something right about this prayer. We should find comfort and help at church, though indirectly. But it is God and not the pastor who is "our refuge and strength, a very present help in trouble" (Ps. 46:1). "Our help is in the name of the LORD, who made heaven and earth" (Ps. 124:8), not in the name of our local parish.

But when that kind of prayer dominates our thinking, it all but obliterates our ability to see the church collectively as the "body of Christ" (1 Cor. 12:12–31); as the "household of God" and as a "holy temple in the Lord" (Eph. 2:19–22); as "living stones . . . built into a spiritual house, to be a holy priesthood, . . . a chosen race, a royal priesthood, a holy nation, God's own people" (1 Pet. 2:4–9).[13] This last reference to the people of God evokes the key formula of the covenant relation between God and the people of God: "I will be their God, and they shall be my people" (Jer. 31:31–34; see also Heb. 8:8–13).[14]

The missional character of the church is also likely to get lost in the shuffle. It's all about me and my needs, or perhaps those of

12. See Christopher Lasch, *Haven in a Heartless World: The Family Besieged* (New York: Basic Books, 1977).

13. And perhaps the bride of Christ (see Rev. 19:7–9).

14. For this way of thinking in relation to the old covenant, see Exod. 6:6–7; 19:4–6; Deut. 4:20; 7:6–11; 14:2; 27:1–10; 29:12–15; Josh. 24:1–28. For an attempt to see the concept of covenant as the basic category of biblical religion, see Merold Westphal, *God, Guilt, and Death: An Existential Phenomenology of Religion* (Bloomington: Indiana University Press, 1984), chap. 11.

my family. If it is to be faithful to its biblical roots, the church as a communal conversation about the Bible will have to make a decisive break with the atomistic, instrumental ethos of American society, which is a confluence of traditions in whose eddies we find ourselves always already swirling. The corporate body will be the interpreter in a more fundamental way than the individual member, and the goal of interpretation will be a deeper understanding of what it means to be the people of God as a worshiping, praying, witnessing, and serving community and what it means to be a person of faith who belongs to that people. Perhaps this is part of what it means "that no prophecy of scripture is a matter of one's own interpretation" (2 Pet. 1:20).

There is another feature of political liberalism, however, that might be helpful in thinking about the church as an ongoing hermeneutical conversation. It comes to clearest expression in the most recent systematic formulation of the theory, that of John Rawls. Political liberalism seeks to specify the conditions "for society to be a fair and stable system of cooperation between free and equal citizens who are deeply divided by the reasonable comprehensive doctrines they affirm." The fundamental condition is that "the basic structure of society is regulated by a political conception of justice" that is "the focus of an overlapping consensus of reasonable comprehensive doctrines."[15]

Understanding the key terms here is crucial. A comprehensive doctrine is what is often called a worldview (*Weltanschauung*). It provides answers to (many, even most of) the metaphysical and moral questions in terms of which we understand who we are and how we should live our lives. It can be quite explicit or merely implicit. It can be secular or religious.

There are two important things to note here. First, Rawls assumes that in an open, democratic society, citizens will be "deeply divided" by holding comprehensive doctrines that are incompatible and irreconcilable with one another. Remembering the emergence of liberalism from Europe's post-Reformation religious pluralism and its violence, Rawls recognizes that this division will be among com-

---

15. John Rawls, *Political Liberalism*, expanded ed. (New York: Columbia University Press, 2005), 44. In this volume, Rawls restates and revises the notion of justice as fairness that he developed in *A Theory of Justice* (Cambridge, MA: Harvard University Press, 1971). Its details do not concern us here.

peting religious comprehensive doctrines but also between religious and secular worldviews and among various secular ones.

Second, political liberalism is not itself a comprehensive doctrine. It affirms certain political values but has no comprehensive morality. It has no view about the relative importance of political values and other values, or, in other words, it offers no account of the highest good.[16] It is neutral with regard to both religious and secular answers to such questions, so while it secularizes the political sphere in important respects, it does not do so by opposing religious doctrines. It is not a secular humanism. Moreover, it lacks the metaphysical and epistemological commitments of a comprehensive doctrine. It is not a theory about what it is to be a person or a human self but only what it is to be a citizen, and it recognizes that to talk about citizenship and its values is to speak abstractly, to focus on one aspect of what is always a more complete, more concrete totality of a human person.

In stating the goal of liberalism as peaceful cooperation rather than merely peaceful coexistence, Rawls assigns to liberal democracy the task of providing citizens with a sense of belonging together, a sense of being on the same team, that is as deep as their differences at the level of comprehensive doctrines. This can be possible only on the basis of an "overlapping consensus of reasonable comprehensive doctrines."

To be reasonable, a comprehensive doctrine need not be true or even probably true. In this context, reasonableness is about the "how" and not the "what" of the doctrine. It is reasonable if those who hold it are not willing to impose its vision and its values on others by means of political power. Competition among comprehensive doctrines occurs in the marketplace of ideas, and this is to be a radically free market so far as the state is concerned. The government's involvement is only to protect the freedom and openness of that space, not to be one of the competitors.

We come finally to the concept that is crucial for our purposes, that of overlapping consensus. It signifies a region of agreement in the midst

---

16. This is why it can be said that for liberalism the right is prior to the good, for it rests on a narrowly *political* conception of justice that is not dependent on any comprehensive concept of the good life and is thus neutral with regard to competing views of that matter. It does affirm various *political* goods, but these represent a "thin" theory of the good. See Rawls, *Theory of Justice*, chaps. 7, 9; and Rawls, *Political Liberalism*, lecture 5.

of disagreement. Consider figure 10.1. The three circles, A, B, and C, overlap in two ways. Areas a, b, and c represent partial overlap. Area a falls within circles B and C but is eccentric to circle A. Similarly, b falls within A and C but is outside B, and c is part of A and B but beyond the pale of C. Overlapping consensus (OC), by contrast, represents a complete overlap. It is an area that falls within all three circles.

FIGURE **10.1**

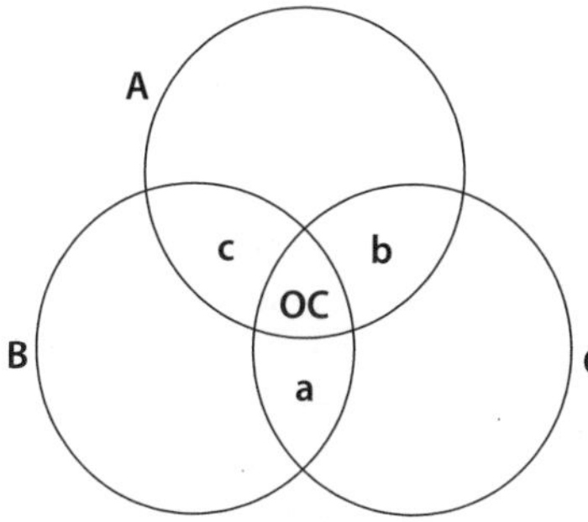

Rawls assumes that in an open society there will be far more than three competing comprehensive doctrines, and he hopes that most of these will be reasonable in his sense of the term. But we can understand the structure he has in mind by simplifying a bit. Let A represent a religiously conservative worldview; let B represent a religiously liberal worldview; and let C represent a secular worldview. These may well overlap in the modes suggested by a, b, and c. Thus c may represent, among other things, an agreement on the existence of God and the importance of prayer and worship. By contrast, area a may represent an agreement about the limits within which stem-cell research and abortion are *morally* permissible.

But it is OC that is crucial for Rawls. To repeat, the possibility "for society to be a fair and stable system of cooperation between free and equal citizens who are deeply divided by the reasonable comprehensive doctrines they affirm" requires that "the basic structure of society is regulated by a political conception of justice" that is "the focus of an overlapping consensus of reasonable comprehensive doctrines."[17] What liberal democracy requires is that all or most

17. Rawls, *Political Liberalism*, 44.

comprehensive doctrines held by its citizens provide warrant for a political conception of justice that will be the common norm for the basic structures of society. This conception—expressed abstractly at the level of principle (ideals) and more concretely, perhaps in a constitution (operative procedures)—is shared by those who differ deeply on many other issues.

It is important to Rawls that this warrant is not merely that of a modus vivendi, an "I'll scratch your back if you scratch mine" compromise in which the parties are each concerned with their own welfare. This is the mentality of the cold war, in which each side said, in effect, "I won't bomb you if you don't bomb me." For Rawls, political liberalism signifies a consensus in which all (or most) citizens share the view that it is both right and good, and thus intrinsically valuable, for others to have the rights of free and equal citizenship as fully as they do themselves. This shared value puts them all on the same team, makes them part of the same family.[18] Rawls hopes that some conception of political justice can find warrant in religiously conservative worldviews, in religiously liberal worldviews, and in various secular worldviews, thereby creating the needed OC.

Similarly, Jürgen Habermas, who identifies himself as a political liberal, asks "whether a society with a plurality of world views can achieve a normative stabilization—that is, something that goes beyond a mere *modus vivendi*" in view of the fact that "liberal societal structures are dependent on the solidarity of their citizens." Citizens in the liberal state can be expected to use their rights "not only in what they rightly take to be their own interests, but also with an orientation to the common good," even where that involves "sacrifices that promote common interests."[19]

To see the possible relevance of this model for Christian hermeneutics, we need only let the circles of the diagram represent disagreements within the Christian church. Each different theology would be a different comprehensive doctrine, and there is no shortage of candidates. We could, for example, let the circles broadly represent

18. Back in the 1960s, when the United States was torn apart by conflict over Vietnam, civil rights, black power, and so forth, the late Rev. William Sloane Coffin Jr. used to repeat, almost as a mantra, "We have more in common than in conflict."

19. Jürgen Habermas and Joseph Ratzinger (Pope Benedict XVI), *The Dialectics of Secularization: On Reason and Religion*, ed. Florian Schuller, trans. Brian McNeil, CRV (San Francisco: Ignatius, 2006), 22, 30. On this theme of solidarity, see also ibid., 29–34, 45–49.

the Orthodox, Roman Catholic, and Protestant traditions.[20] Once again we can easily find the partial overlaps represented by a, b, and c, and once again we can find an OC.

There are and have been various attempts to articulate the OC of the Christian churches. Here are three examples: reference to the ecumenical creeds, C. S. Lewis's notion of "mere Christianity," and the attempt in the early years of the twentieth century to specify the "fundamentals" of the faith. This means that in the conflict of interpretations the content of the OC will itself be a matter of debate, just as there will be debate about matters not seen as candidates for this role even by their defenders. This was already the case for political liberalism, for while Rawls thinks his theory of justice is the best one to represent the OC of political liberalism, he recognizes that there are competing theories that could also play that role.

This epistemic humility may be at least as important in the religious domain as in the political one. The temptation is always to think that my (or our) comprehensive doctrine (or at least most of my theology) should be the OC in terms of which Christianity should be defined. Our diagram, the model of political liberalism, and Gadamer's hermeneutics suggests the possibility of a more ecumenical approach. If interpretation, like performance and translation, always involves saying the same thing differently (chaps. 7 and 9), and if, correspondingly, interpretation is always productive and not merely reproductive (chap. 5), then we should expect difference. And if, by analogy with the six blind men and the elephant (chap. 1), any finite perspective enables us at best to grasp part but not all of the truth, then we should not be surprised if some of these differences are irreconcilable.

But if we can look for and seek to articulate an overlapping consensus, we may find various modes of cooperative life together as friends and not enemies; we may find our disagreements are more like family quarrels than all-out warfare. We may be less inclined to religiously legitimated violence and to linguistically violent religious rhetoric, language that seeks to denigrate, manipulate, or seduce our opponents.[21] We may find our agreement about the importance

20. Broadening the conversation, we could let A, B, and C represent the three Abrahamic monotheisms: Judaism, Christianity, and Islam. But our present concern is intra-Christian conversation.

21. Violent religious rhetoric both reflects and reinforces the violent political rhetoric of bitter partisanship that dominates the political debate in the United States as this chapter is being written.

of baptism and the Eucharist (Lord's Supper, Communion) more important than our disagreement over infant baptism versus believer baptism or the exact significance of the words "This is my body," and we may be less inclined to close Communion to those who do not interpret it exactly as we do. Political liberalism provides for the Christian churches whose interpretations of the Bible overlap and diverge from a model for a possible solidarity amidst differences.

Communitarianism: A Model for the Church?

The liberal-communitarian debate is one of two ships passing in the night and not making real contact, for the assumption is false that they give alternative answers to the same questions. We can take John Rawls and Alasdair MacIntyre as paradigmatic representatives of the liberal and communitarian traditions, respectively. But the latter lets the cat out of the bag by quoting a passage from the end of *After Virtue* in the very opening paragraph of its sequel, *Whose Justice? Which Rationality?*

> My own conclusion is very clear. It is that on the one hand we still, in spite of the efforts of three centuries of moral philosophy and one of sociology, lack any coherent rationally defensible statement of a liberal individualist point of view; and that, on the other hand, the Aristotelian tradition can be restated in a way that restores intelligibility and rationality to our moral and social attitudes and commitments.[22]

MacIntyre's concern is with the intelligibility, rationality, and justification of our moral values. This concern makes it clear that communitarianism is what Rawls calls a comprehensive doctrine or, to be more precise, a metatheory about comprehensive doctrines. Drawing on a tradition that stretches back through Hegel to Aristotle, communitarianism argues that a coherent moral life requires what Rawls would call a comprehensive doctrine, a worldview that includes commitments on issues from which political liberalism deliberately abstains.[23] Such doctrines will have three important features.

---

22. MacIntyre, *After Virtue*, 241; Alasdair MacIntyre, *Whose Justice? Which Rationality?* (Notre Dame, IN: University of Notre Dame Press, 1988), ix.

23. Communitarian complaints that liberalism fails to give a comprehensive account of what it is to be a human self simply miss the point, since liberalism does not

First, a communitarian worldview will include a theory of the good, namely, an account of the highest good or goods for human life and some sort of comparative, hierarchical analysis of greater and lesser goods. Second, the comprehensive doctrine will include a comprehensive account of the virtues, not restricting itself to the civic virtues, and it will articulate the vision of the human self presupposed by these practices and habits of character. Third, it will recognize that the virtues essential to the good life will be rooted in specific communities and their historical traditions.[24] It will not appeal to a "pure," unsituated, universal reason of the sort aspired to by what MacIntyre calls the Enlightenment Project.[25]

We can perhaps get a handle on what communitarian thinking is like with help from Glenn Heck. During my junior high days, Heck was a youth leader in our church and a school principal. He once asked a group of us how we would identify ourselves if we could say only three things in introducing ourselves. I don't remember my answer to his question, but I remember his:

I am Glenn Heck.
I am an American.
I am a Christian.

This is first-class communitarian thinking. The use of the first person pronoun and the first name indicate that he takes himself to be a unique individual and not merely a function of some larger system. But at the same time he acknowledges that he is that individual precisely by virtue of his participation in a variety of communities, their traditions, and their practices. It is through socialization that he has become himself. The first of these communities is the Heck family, nuclear and, quite possibly, extended. The second of these is America, and this involves a rich and complex mixture of traditions and practices that are political, economic, educational, and cultural. Finally, as a Christian, although he may well say he has a personal

---

purport to give such a theory. A good example of this misunderstanding can be found in Michael J. Sandel, *Liberalism and the Limits of Justice* (New York: Cambridge University Press, 1982).

24. The emphasis on community and character in the work of Stanley Hauerwas indicates that he seeks to develop a Christian version of communitarian theory.

25. In the hands of Locke, liberalism belongs to the Enlightenment Project, but Rawls recognizes that liberalism is itself a historically emergent and developing tradition.

relation with God through Jesus Christ and the Holy Spirit, he is no atomic soul communing with God in some ethereal isolation ward. He is a member of the Christian church and, indeed, of a Christian church and is an inheritor of a doubtless complex subset of Christian traditions and practices. It is as a participating member in these communities that his moral values and metaphysical beliefs, including what it is to be a person, make sense and do not seem to be random or arbitrary preferences. It is in relation to these communities (and others, no doubt) that he is *wirkungsgeschichtliches Bewusstsein* (chap. 6).

We seem to be back on Gadamerian soil. Both ontologically and epistemologically, the emphasis is on the individual's contingent embeddedness in particular cultural traditions and practices. These are not necessarily static and fixed. In accordance with Gadamer's "revise-revise-replace" formula (chap. 6), traditions develop over time; it is this flexibility of traditions as they seek to solve problems they could not originally deal with effectively that MacIntyre calls the "rationality of traditions."[26] Moreover, individuals switch allegiances, although such "conversions" may be minor as well as major.[27] Such movement is within and among various traditions, not from this or that tradition to somewhere outside all traditions.

Viewed as a political theory, communitarianism is dangerous, for in such a role it would make the state the principal teacher of morality. Reflecting an anxiety in the face of cultural pluralism and a nostalgia for a more nearly homogeneous society, it forgets the dangers that liberalism was designed to address and opens the way to intolerant and even violent domination of minorities by cultural majorities or even of majorities by militant minorities.

But we are not doing political theory, and in fact communitarianism is a far better model for the church than it is for the state. Churches derive their identity from their theologies, which are comprehensive doctrines with substantial metaphysical and moral dimensions; so they are, from a communitarian perspective, well suited to be the moral teachers of their members and to bear moral witness to the larger society in which they find themselves. If they read their Bible

---

26. MacIntyre, *Whose Justice?* chap. 18.

27. A young woman who grew up in a Presbyterian church told her parents, not too long after enrolling in Calvin College, that she had "converted" to Christian Reformed.

carefully, they will understand that when Jesus said "My kingdom is not from this world" this did not mean that it was only concerned with otherworldly, "spiritual" matters but that it was not to establish itself by means of the sword. Drawing on the rhetoric of Hebrew parallelism, in which the second phrase says the same as the first but differently, as in so many psalms,[28] Jesus is quite clear. "My kingdom is not from this world. If my kingdom were from this world, my followers would be fighting" (John 18:36).[29] Worldly kingdoms establish themselves by military power; the kingdom of God does not.[30]

But there is another kind of violence against which communitarian self-understandings of the church must protect themselves. It is right in the middle of a "communitarian" exhortation to unity in the church as the body of Christ that we read: "But speaking the truth in love, we must grow up in every way into him who is the head, into Christ, from whom the whole body, joined and knit together by every ligament with which it is equipped, as each part is working properly, promotes the body's growth in building itself up in love" (Eph. 4:15–16).

Rhetoric can be as violent as any armaments and speaking the truth (as we understand it—how else could we speak it?) in love so as to build up the body in love is hardly compatible with anathemas that say, directly or indirectly, to those who don't share our particular comprehensive doctrine, "Go to hell!"

We do not have to choose between these two models. Political liberalism can be a model in which we understand ourselves to be *the* church of Jesus Christ, which tries to be one church in spite of an undeniable pluralism of theories and practices. Communitarianism can be a model of the comprehensive integrity of the particular traditions that constitute this plurality and that keep Christianity from being reduced to its least common denominator. With this picture in mind, let us examine the possible analogical usefulness of political liberalism and moral communitarianism in a concrete, theological context.

28. For example, "Bless the LORD, O my soul, and all that is within me, bless his holy name" (Ps. 103:1).

29. Cf. John 18:11: "Jesus said to Peter, 'Put your sword back into its sheath.'"

30. It is helpful here to recall Max Weber's definition of the state: "a human community that (successfully) claims the *monopoly of the legitimate use of physical force* within a given territory" (Weber, "Politics as a Vocation," in *From Max Weber: Essays in Sociology*, ed. and trans. Hans Heinrich Gerth and C. Wright Mills [New York: Oxford University Press, 1946], 78; emphasis in the original).

11

The Church as Conversation

Ecumenical Conversation: A Case Study

We are thinking of the church as the ongoing conversation in which the Bible is interpreted, the double conversation between interpreters and the text and the conversation among interpreters; we are exploring political liberalism and moral communitarianism as heuristic devices for our ecclesiology; and, for the moment, we are turning our attention to an ecumenical conversation among theologians, who are scholars whose interpretations of both Scripture and tradition are written in books and articles.

On October 31, 1999, in Augsburg, Germany, the World Lutheran Federation and representatives of the Roman Catholic Church signed the Joint Declaration on the Doctrine of Justification.[1] Against the background of Vatican II and after nearly thirty-five years of dialogue and preliminary drafts, in which then-Cardinal Ratzinger played an important role, section 4 of the Declaration affirmed the following agreements:

1. "We confess together that all persons depend completely on the saving grace of God for their salvation."

1. *Joint Declaration on the Doctrine of Justification* (Grand Rapids: Eerdmans, 2000).

2. "We confess together that God forgives sin by grace and at the same time frees human beings from sin's enslaving power and imparts the gift of new life in Christ."

3. "We confess together that sinners are justified by faith in the saving action of God in Christ."

4. "We confess together that in baptism the Holy Spirit unites one with Christ, justifies and truly renews the person. But the justified must all through life constantly look to God's unconditional justifying grace."

5. "We confess together that persons are justified by faith in the Gospel 'apart from works prescribed by the law.'"

6. "We confess together that the faithful can rely on the mercy and promises of God."

7. "We confess together that good works—a Christian life lived in faith, hope and love—follow justification and are its fruits."[2]

After centuries of polemics and hostility, whose tone and substance were set by the writings of Martin Luther and the Council of Trent, this is a remarkable result. It is important to see both what it isn't and what it is.

First, it does not have structural, organic union of the churches involved as either its goal or its result.

Second, as one Catholic commentator points out, "Ratification of this document does not bring Lutherans and Romans into full communion with each other" (*RPT* 59). Lutherans, for example, are not thereby made welcome at the Catholic Eucharist.

Third, as the document itself and the commentators point out, it does not represent full agreement among the signatories about all issues surrounding the question of justification, much less many other issues about which the two traditions have disagreed. Important theological differences remain among the participants, and outside the community of participants but within the Lutheran and Catholic churches there are those on both sides who see the Joint

2. Cited in David E. Aune, ed., *Rereading Paul Together: Protestant and Catholic Perspectives on Justification* (Grand Rapids: Baker Academic, 2006), 35–36. Henceforth *RPT*. This volume grew out of a conference sponsored by Notre Dame and Valparaiso universities in 2002 and contains discussion by five Catholic and five Protestant (four Lutheran and one Presbyterian, who teaches at Valparaiso) scholars on various aspects of the ongoing conversation.

Declaration as a sellout, convinced that their side compromised too much.[3] Section 5 ¶40 asserts, "Therefore the Lutheran and the Catholic explications of justification are *in their differences* open to one another and do not destroy the consensus regarding basic truths" (*RPT* 36; emphasis added). It represents a "differentiated consensus" (*RPT* 42) that does not try to hide the fact that "Lutherans and Catholics view many topics through different lenses" (*RPT* 48). Thus the commentators point out the different languages in which the two sides operate: the Catholics in scholastic, metaphysical language, the Lutherans in experiential, relational language (*RPT* 38). Commentators also note the different theologies that are the context for reflection on justification, a theology of baptism in the Catholic case and of penance in the Lutheran case (*RPT* 47).

Fourth, the reference to a "consensus regarding basic truths" does not represent an attempt to define the identity of either tradition in terms of some lowest common denominator. There is no suggestion that the two are essentially identical and only accidentally different.

If these are dimensions of unity that the Joint Declaration does not achieve (or even attempt to achieve), what can be said positively about what it does accomplish? First, without even trying to paper over significant remaining disagreements, it is an expression of *unity* in difference. It refers to the "notable convergence" it represents (*RPT* 35). As one commentator puts it, the Joint Declaration is "the acknowledgment that the unity of faith can be expressed in different languages and in various theological forms with particular emphases" (*RPT* 48). Second, one aspect of this unity is the understanding that at least on the issue of justification the differences that remain, while real, are no longer church dividing (*RPT* 46, 62). Third, a consequence of the previous point and perhaps the most immediate of its operational imperatives is the cessation of violent rhetoric. The vitriolic language, the condemnations, the demonizing of the other side as an enemy of the cross of Christ are no longer warranted by the differences that remain (*RPT* 29–30). In other words, no more anathemas (*RPT* 40).

Returning to the question of political liberalism and moral communitarianism as possible analogs for the church as a hermeneuti-

3. Not surprisingly, one Web site from outside either tradition ran the headline, "Liberal Lutherans and Roman Catholics Agree to Deny the Gospel" (*RPT* 36).

cal conversation, what can be said? First, political liberalism looks good. What the Joint Declaration represents is a conversation that discovered/created an overlapping consensus. (It is also an example of what Gadamer would call the fusion of horizons.) In terms of the diagram in chapter 10, if we let A be the Catholics and B be the Lutherans, then c represents the consensus of the Joint Declaration. Since other Christian traditions have not signed on, there is no OC, no all-inclusive overlapping consensus. But a formula of concord between these two communions on this crucial bone of contention is no trivial result.

Second, both as intention and as result there is a significant stepping back from the resort to violence as a method of dealing with differences. Political liberalism was born as an attempt to overcome all too literally violent wars of religion and religious persecution. Partly due to its success, Rawls is able to describe as "rational" those comprehensive views whose holders don't merely refrain from violent imposition but also refrain from imposition by means of political power. In the context of the Joint Declaration we can perhaps substitute "faithful" for "rational." The Catholic and Lutheran comprehensive doctrines are "faithful" in the relevant formal sense to the degree that they take on themselves not only the double self-denying ordinance just described (no imposition by force of arms or by political power) but also the refusal to treat their other as an enemy to be subdued by means of violent and vitriolic rhetoric, condemnations, and anathemas.

Third, the peace hereby established, fragile as it may be, is not a cold war modus vivendi. The entire spirit of the Joint Declaration is to highlight the sense in which the two parties belong together, belong to something bigger than either. Just as citizenship in political liberalism is not just a contractual compromise but a celebration of shared values of liberty and justice for all (however imperfectly enacted in practice), so believers shaped by and living in different traditions can here celebrate their joint affirmation: "Together we confess: By grace alone, in faith in Christ's saving work and not because of any merit on our part, we are accepted by God and receive the Holy Spirit, who renews our hearts while equipping and calling us to good works" (§15, *RPT* 35).

At the same time, the communitarian model has not been eliminated as a useful heuristic. First and foremost, the Joint Declaration recognizes the reality of the type of comprehensive doctrines communitarian thought finds indispensable: rich networks of beliefs and practices rooted in traditions that can give reasonably coherent meaning to the whole of life. Both Catholic and Lutheran thought extend beyond the area of overlap outlined, and there is no suggestion that Catholic families and churches should not raise their children as Catholics and similarly for Lutherans. Put a bit differently, there is no suggestion that the concrete identity of a Catholic or Lutheran believer should be extracted from or reduced to the area of consensus, however important that may be against centuries of mutual recrimination.

Second, moral communitarianism is a form of virtue ethics, one that stresses the formation of character in the light of comprehensive doctrines and the traditions in which they dwell. The ecumenical conversation presupposed by and presented in the Joint Declaration involves several important virtues. In this respect it exhibits the Aristotelian dimension we find in MacIntyre and Gadamer's joint emphasis on practical wisdom, which makes theory ancillary to practice.

First and foremost is epistemic or hermeneutical humility. Without trying to flee from tradition, there is a genuine concern not to idolize one's own tradition. This kind of conversation requires participants to "be open to considering resources from other traditions and limitations within its own tradition" (*RPT* 65). Because of their comprehensive coherence, communities deeply rooted in a particular tradition need to hear the voices of outsiders. Scripture is supposed to be a mirror in which we can see ourselves as we really are and as we can and should become (James 1:22–25). But ironically, Scripture can all too easily become the wrong kind of mirror.

> When distortions of character enter and deeply permeate the life of any Christian community, that community loses its ability to read Scripture in ways that would challenge and correct its character. Scripture simply becomes a mirror reflecting a community's self-deceptions back to itself disguised as the word of God.[4]

We can recall George Tyrell's claim that the Christ of Adolf Harnack's famous *What Is Christianity?* was only the reflection of Har-

---

4. Stephen E. Fowl and L. Gregory Jones, *Reading in Communion: Scripture and Ethics in Christian Life* (Grand Rapids: Eerdmans, 1991), 99. Fowl and Jones argue that "communities which are closed in on themselves may require the presence of prophets whose voices they are unwilling to hear" (ibid., 2).

nack's own face, "seen at the bottom of a deep well" (chap. 4 above). No doubt the deep well is meant to symbolize tunnel vision in its perpendicular mode. Such vision can be the result of either our finitude, as with the blind men and the elephant (chap. 1), or our fallenness, since in our sinfulness we "suppress the truth" (Rom. 1:18). *It is important for the church not to read this passage from Romans as if it applied only to nonbelievers.*

Scripture itself is supposed to be an outsider that can "challenge and correct our character," both individually and collectively. Ultimately it is the work of the Holy Spirit to help us see what we are supposed to see in the Bible, but the Holy Spirit can and often does use human messengers, which is what the prophets, the apostles, and the Incarnation itself are all about. If God can use Balaam's ass to help him see the error of his ways (Num. 22), and if, as I have argued, God can use Marx, Nietzsche, and Freud to be prophetic voices to Christendom,[5] then surely God can use Christians from other traditions to help us better hear, understand, and embody Scripture—if we have the humility to let them, to listen and to learn from them.

This points to a second crucial virtue: good listening. We are reminded of the couple visiting a marriage counselor (chap. 9) when we encounter this hermeneutical rule for ecumenical conversation: "you may not condemn another's position unless and until you have stated the opposing position in language that the opponent/partner affirms and approves" (*RPT* 39). We might call good listening a skill, but it is better described as a virtue, for it rests less on intellectual ability and more on an attitude of openness that is not just willing but eager to let the others have their say—in their language and from their perspective. Otherwise they are reduced to the status of a self-justifying mirror in which we see ourselves as right because they are wrong and we are different from them. The exposure of this self-deception is the heart and soul of Nietzsche's possible role as a prophet to the churches.

Third, there is the virtue of friendship. In this context this means seeing those from other traditions not first and foremost as those with whom we disagree but as fellow Christians who are trying to be faithful to the gospel. Thus one commentator writes, "I myself

5. Merold Westphal, *Suspicion and Faith: The Religious Uses of Modern Atheism* (New York: Fordham University Press, 1998).

suspect that diplomatic advances—whether in the geo-political or ecclesial variety—are forged as much by personal friendships across boundaries of entrenched alienation as by any other factor. Hence friendship is not only a result of such work, but is perhaps also its precondition" (*RPT* 132).[6] A beautiful example of such friendship is found in the conversation between Marcus J. Borg and N. T. Wright about the historical Jesus.[7]

A final way in which the communitarian model can be helpful is in its perspectivism. Gadamer's hermeneutics, with its emphasis on our embeddedness in particular traditions, is a reminder that we never see things from either everywhere or nowhere. We are always located somewhere. In harmony with this, MacIntyre's communitarianism rejects the "Enlightenment Project" of extracting ourselves from our sociality and our historicity and emphasizes the positive role that tradition can play in giving coherent meaning to our lives. The perspectival character of this perspective comes to light in the title of a sequel to *After Virtue*, namely, *Whose Justice? Which Rationality?* Here is the acknowledgment that different traditions have not only different conceptions of justice but also different conceptions of rationality. Substantive debates cannot necessarily be resolved by appeal to "Reason" as criterion because the very meaning of reason and thus of the operative criteria differ from one community of discourse to another, especially as we move through historical time. Nor are Christians who appeal to "Scripture" as the highest criterion, right and proper as that is, immune from the questions, "Whose Scripture?" "The Bible according to whom?"

A particularly interesting perspective on this perspectivism emerges in one of the commentaries on the Joint Declaration. It is not about the differing perspectives on justification but about differing perspectives on a closely related matter. It is pointed out that the effects of the Christ-event are summed up by Paul

6. For a similar suggestion about the hermeneutical significance of friendship, see Fowl and Jones, *Reading in Communion*, 2. Commentators have suggested that the paralyzing partisanship in Congress in recent years is largely because members are at home three days a week (raising money for the next election) and have no time to form friendships across the aisle.

7. Marcus J. Borg and N. T. Wright, *The Meaning of Jesus: Two Visions* (New York: HarperSanFrancisco, 1999). The focus here is on disagreement, in spite of significant overlap, but the spirit of friendship and mutual respect pervades.

under ten different images: justification, salvation, reconciliation, expiation, redemption, freedom, sanctification, transformation, new creation, and glorification. Each of these images expresses a distinctive aspect of christocentric soteriology. . . . If the Christ-event is conceived of as a decahedron, a ten-sided solid figure, one can understand how Paul, gazing at one panel of it, might use one image to express its effect (e.g., he justified us), whereas he might use another image when gazing at another panel (he reconciled us). Each of the ten panels would be expressing only one aspect of the whole. (*RPT* 82; cf. 144)

When reference is made to the "multifaceted soteriology in Pauline thought" (*RPT* 83), the suggestion is clear that the decahedron in question is a diamond—a brilliant, glistening gem. A respondent summarizes the message of this metaphor as follows: "If you emphasize justification too much, you risk diminishing the Christ-event and distorting Paul" (*RPT* 100). As in the case of the six blind men from Hindustan (chap. 1), where we stand when we look shows itself in what we are able to see and what we have a hard time seeing, if we see it at all, and there is no church tradition that does not have its own distinctive "canon within the canon."

Another example of the same sort focuses attention on the debate about whether justification means being declared righteous or being made righteous. Lutherans have traditionally emphasized the former, but, rejecting the notion that this is an either/or proposition, the Joint Declaration affirms, "to be justified [also] means that out of unrighteous people righteous people are made or regenerated. . . . *Scripture speaks both ways*" (*RPT* 112; emphasis added; cf. 84–85). To emphasize one to the (virtual) exclusion of the other is to distort the truth. The way to objectivity is not to flee perspectives but to multiply them.

Conversations Closer to Home

Rereading Paul Together (and perhaps the Joint Declaration itself)[8] might well be made required reading in divinity schools and theological seminaries, not just for its contribution to substantive theological matters but especially for the light it throws on theological

8. See note 1 of this chapter.

conversations with outsiders, those who come from traditions different from our own. It may be that academic theologians are best equipped to participate in such ecumenical conversations, but if the ideal of a theologically educated clergy is to mean more than reading a few books on church growth and parish management, the (ongoing) formation of pastors should include learning the hermeneutical humility that recognizes the limits of one's own traditions by learning to recognize and treasure the resources to be found in other traditions. Of course pastors should know their own tradition thoroughly, but the deliberate attempt to learn from other traditions might well be conceived as an intellectual virtue and a moral duty.

One can even imagine (dream? fantasize?) of local ministerial associations that aspire to more than the B and B (bragging and bitching) into which they so easily degenerate. They might sometimes be conversations in which pastors from varying theological, sociological, ethnic, and racial perspectives and experiences share their insights into biblical texts, especially those that underlie separations and suspicions among them. If carried out in a spirit of friendship and mutual respect, they might discover more common ground than they suspected, and even if this does not happen, they might learn from one another.

But the double conversation with the biblical text and with other traditions cannot be the exclusive task of an ecclesiastical elite, namely, theologians and pastors. If we take seriously the Reformation theme of the priesthood of all believers, we will have to acknowledge that hermeneutical conversation is the privilege and responsibility of the laity as well. We can consider three levels at which the Bible is read by the laity, remembering that to read is to interpret: the individual, the family, and the congregation.

If we are really serious about the claim that the Bible is the Word of God and that it properly becomes the Word of God again and again as the Holy Spirit speaks to us through Scripture, then every believer should be in regular conversation with the text. Conversation is a two-way street, in this case listening for God's voice and responding to what we hear in praise, thanksgiving, repentance, and obedient action. We are to be hearers of the word and doers of the word, those who perform and embody it, for to hear without doing is precisely not to hear.

The layperson is usually not in a very good position to ask the first question of the double hermeneutics proposed above: what did the human author say to the original community of readers or hearers? This requires a significant measure of scholarly expertise.[9] So focus will be on the second question: what is God saying to me here and now in this passage? The ancient tradition of *lectio divina* can be a help here.

Lectio. Read the passage carefully, paying special attention to words or phrases that jump out at you. Use your imagination. In a narrative passage, try to picture the scene and yourself as one of the participants, for example, the returning prodigal, the elder brother, the father, or one of the servants. How would you feel? What would you say? In a nonnarrative text, such as one of the epistles, imagine yourself as one of the original addressees. What is your church life like? In the psalms, try to make this your own prayer; then ask who in the world might pray it even more deeply; then, following an old tradition, think of Jesus as praying the psalm. There are a lot of enemies in the psalms. Ask yourself: Who are the enemies here and now from whom I seek deliverance? How are the world, the flesh, and the devil enemies in my life at present?

Read the passage again. After using your imagination to place yourself within its world, ask the crucial question: what is God saying to me through this text today?

The four questions suggested earlier by Luther (chap. 9) may be helpful here. What am I to believe? What am I to do? Of what am I to repent? For what am I to give thanks?

Meditatio. Meditate on what you have seen, smelled, felt, and, above all, heard in your reading. Dwell. Linger. Abide. Chew the cud. Having entered into the text, let it wash over you so that it becomes the place where you *are* more fully than the room in which you sit.

Oratio. Pray. Having listened for God's word in God's word, respond. Tell God what's on your mind. Tell God everything, including the intruding thoughts that keep distracting you from attention to

---

9. But help with this aspect can be found in such accessible commentaries as William Barclay's *The Daily Study Bible Series* (Philadelphia: Westminster, 1955–76). Three steps might be helpful: (1) read the passage and meditate on it; (2) read Barclay's commentary; then (3) reread the passage and meditate on it in the light of the commentary. Under constraints of time, this can be spread over two or three days if necessary. It's about hearing, not about haste.

the text. Say "Thank you." Say "I'm sorry." Ask for help in understanding and embodying this text.

Contemplatio. Contemplate. Remind yourself that in this conversation with the text you are having a conversation with God, that you are in the presence of God, and that by grace through faith God is lovingly with you. As in *meditatio*, let this mutual presence be the place where, for these moments, you consciously dwell.

There is, of course, nothing magical or mandatory about this approach. What is important is the regular, devotional conversation with the Bible in which one listens attentively to hear what God is saying here and now, in and through this text.

The family is another site for biblical interpretation. Christian parents can and should be pastors and teachers to their children, bringing them up in the "discipline and instruction of the Lord" (Eph. 6:4). If it is important to read to them and to teach them how to read, as many parents do, can it be any less important to read the Bible to them and teach them how to read it?

My own first exposure to the Bible came from a children's story Bible from which my mother read to us (along with Uncle Wiggley and *The Prince and the Pin Elves*). We didn't have television or Dr. Seuss, so the world of my imagination was largely the world of biblical narrative. I don't remember my mother ever putting it to us just this way, but I can imagine a family bedtime ritual consisting of Bible stories along with the question, especially as the children get a bit older, "What do you think God is saying to us in this story?" Like prayer, hermeneutical habits can never be formed too early. If pastors have theologians to help them, and lay adults have pastors, why should children not have parents to be their theologians and pastors, exposing them to the text, teaching what kinds of questions to ask, and making suggestions about the kinds of answers to look for?

Can we imagine an extension of this model into the youth programs of our churches? Competing with popular culture makes this dimension of the church's ministry enormously difficult (possibly more difficult than the adult dimension). But who knows what interest Bible study might hold for teens if they were encouraged to talk about the Bible on the assumption that God has a great deal to say to them here and now through its stories, poetry, prophetic preaching, and apostolic letters—especially if the adults in the congregation, including their parents, were setting the example.

We can now turn our attention to the conversation about Scripture among the lay adults of a local congregation. What would happen in a congregation in which during the hour before the Sunday morning worship service (or some time during the week) the congregation met in small groups to share their insights on the text for the morning's sermon, asking "What is God saying to us in this week's text?" and offering answers from their varying perspectives and experiences. One immediate result, I suspect, is that it would put a certain pressure on the pastor to pay close attention to the text on which, presumably, the sermon is based. This would be a useful guard against lapsing into good, sound, biblical generalities with little or no visible connection with the text, which thereby tend to degenerate into platitudes. The congregation—pastor and laity together—would be focused on listening for what God is saying not just here and now but in this particular text.

There is a variation on this particular suggestion that may have some merit. In churches that follow a lectionary, there is a widespread habit of preaching primarily or even exclusively on the Gospel text. In many churches that do not follow a lectionary, there is a widespread habit of preaching predominantly from the Epistles. Important facets of the biblical diamond are ignored in this way. A possible corrective would be in the first kind of church to have the congregation in small groups listening for God's word in the Epistles and in the second kind of church in the Gospels. Perhaps it would even be possible to bring the Old Testament into the picture.

It just might be that the vitality of a local congregation depends less on the prevailing *theory* of how the Bible is the Word of God than on the widespread *practice* of treating it as such in individual, family, and congregational readings that seek to hear what the Spirit says to the churches through the Word.

12

Transcendence, Revelation, and Community

The Dialectical Tension of Human and Divine

In presenting Gadamerian hermeneutics I have spoken of the Bible as the "classic" text of the Christian church, linking it for hermeneutical purposes with other classics such as Shakespeare and the United States Constitution. In important respects, interpreting the Bible is like interpreting other texts of major cultural significance.

But if the Bible is not less than the church's classic text, it is surely more than this at the same time. It is the Word of God. The gospel of God was "promised beforehand through his prophets in the holy scriptures" (Rom. 1:2).

> The household of God [is] built upon the foundation of the apostles and prophets, with Christ Jesus himself as the cornerstone. (Eph. 2:19–20)

> In former generations this mystery was not made known to humankind, as it has now been revealed to his holy apostles and prophets by the Spirit. (Eph. 3:5)

> Long ago God spoke to our ancestors in many and various ways by the prophets, but in these last days he has spoken to us by a Son. (Heb. 1:1–2)

First of all you must understand this, that no prophecy of scripture
is a matter of one's own interpretation, because no prophecy ever
came by human will, but men and women moved by the Holy Spirit
spoke from God. (2 Pet. 1:20–21)

To speak of prophets and apostles and even of a Son is to speak of
the double nature of Scripture. Those through whom the Bible has
come to us were most certainly human, humans who had particular
interests and concerns related to their immediate circumstances. In
exploring the *Sitz im Leben* of these writers, biblical scholarship
has shown us the many ways in which they were *wirkungsgeschichtliches Bewusstsein* (chap. 6). An indispensable step in interpreting
the Bible is to understand as much as possible about the context and
the agenda of the biblical writers.

But to speak of those whose words and deeds are recorded and
those who did the recording as prophets and apostles is to say that
they are more than bearers of human traditions, even creative and
original thinkers within the context of those traditions. It is to say
that God spoke and still speaks through them. This is what it means
to say that the Bible is the Word of God. Thus the need for the double
hermeneutic that asks: What speech acts *did* the human writer perform in writing, say, the history of the kings of Israel or the Epistle
to Titus? What speech acts *does* God perform in addressing these
writings to us now as the Word of God? (see chap. 3).

The church shares this dialectical nature with its classic text.[1]
For as the church at Ephesus was told, "you are citizens with the
saints and also members of the household of God, built upon the
foundation of the apostles and prophets, with Christ Jesus himself
as the cornerstone" (Eph. 2:19–20). As citizens of a new nation, even
a "holy nation" (1 Pet. 2:9), and as members of a family, Christians
belong to groups that are shaped by and are bearers of a variety of
traditions. But they are also the people of God, a new creation that,
like the old creation, has been brought into being and sustained in
its being by God's wise and loving power.

That creative and sustaining power is exercised both indirectly,
through the Bible, and directly, by the Holy Spirit, for the Holy
Spirit not only was directly involved in the creation of the Bible (see

---

1. Dialectic signifies an ongoing tension between opposite elements that can be neither
separated from nor dissolved into each other. Luther's formula *simul justus et peccator*
is a good example, as is the union of the human and divine natures in Christ.

Eph. 3:5 and 2 Pet. 1:20–21 above) but also continues to guide the church in understanding it. Jesus promised that "the Holy Spirit, whom the Father will send in my name, will teach you everything, and remind you of all that I have said to you. . . . When the Spirit of truth comes, he will guide you into all the truth" (John 14:26; 16:13). The formula "Word and Spirit" is the keystone for any biblical hermeneutics.

Of course, this formula is anything but a method. Neither the Word of God nor the Spirit of God would be restricted or confined to the rules and procedures of any human method. But it may seem as if the primarily Gadamerian hermeneutic presented here, with its emphasis on human traditions and human conversations, confines the Word of God too much to human horizons even without being a method. Does hermeneutics muzzle and muffle the divine voice of Scripture? That is the fear that underlies the spurious but understandable wish: "no interpretation needed" (chap. 1).

The first response to this question is to acknowledge that human, all too human, interpretation takes place with or without a hermeneutical theory that notices it. The history of the Christian churches bears eloquent witness to this fact. The second response is to try to think how the divine nature of Scripture lives in dialectical tension not only with its own human origins but also with its ongoing human interpretation.

To speak of the divine nature of Scripture and of the church as a community built on the foundation of Scripture is to speak of revelation, and to speak of revelation is to speak of divine transcendence. The divine voice is not reducible to the human voices that give us Scripture either by writing it or by interpreting it. In this context it is not enough to speak of cosmological transcendence, of God's *being* as "beyond," "outside," or "independent of" the being of the world, the totality of nature and history. It is necessary to speak of God's *actions*, in this case *speech acts*, in and by which God invades the world, or rather dwells in it, for God has never left the world. Divine transcendence is always in a dialectical tension with divine immanence. But human history in its finitude and fallenness is always declaring its self-sufficiency, more or less explicitly. So the divine word is never simply the inner logos of human traditions with their associated practices and ideologies. It always has the character of breaking in from without. Nor is this the case only in relation to the world, as distinct from the church. The church, too, stands under the judgment of Scripture and in need of its guidance. That is the meaning of the Reformed formula: *ecclesia reformata, semper reformanda secundum verbi dei* (the church reformed and always being reformed according to Word of God).

Levinas on Revelation as Transcendence

The Jewish philosopher Emmanuel Levinas can be helpful in understanding the dialectical relation between the human and the divine dimensions of the Bible and its interpretation. He is not speaking about the Bible when he talks about revelation, and it is not even clear that he is speaking about God in any genuinely monotheistic sense. He uses the term *God* a lot, along with such theologically loaded terms as revelation, glory, height, and so forth. Both friends and foes often take this diction to have genuinely theistic meaning, but he often says things that lead to the conclusion that *God* signifies not a personal agent—for example, a speaker, lover, and savior, distinct from all human agents—but rather the depth dimension of other humans by virtue of which I am infinitely and unconditionally responsible to and for them. The face of the other person, especially the widow, the orphan, and the stranger, is the bearer of this depth, this height, this glory; it is the only medium of "revelation."[2] As Levinas put it, "The face speaks."[3]

The voice that speaks in, as, and through the face of the human other[4] is doubly interruptive. It is neither mine nor ours. This voice disturbs *my* natural (not necessarily but possibly evil) preoccupation with *myself* by intruding forcefully and uninvited with the claims of the other for justice. But it equally challenges *our* natural (not necessarily but possibly evil) preoccupation with *our* needs and interests, whether they be of family, class, race, gender, or nation. The widow,

2. I have discussed this ambiguity in Levinas's thought in Merold Westphal, *Levinas and Kierkegaard in Dialogue* (Bloomington: Indiana University Press, 2008), esp. chaps. 3–4.

3. Emmanuel Levinas, *Totality and Infinity: An Essay on Exteriority*, trans. Alphonso Lingis (Pittsburgh: Duquesne University Press, 1969), 66; hereafter *TF*.

4. Levinas uses the abstract term *other* to signify the neighbor of Lev. 19:18 and "one of the least of these who are members of my family" (see Matt. 25). The widow, orphan, and stranger are radically "other" because by their presence, their face, they intrude into my personal and social world, whose natural instinct is to exclude them by ignoring them, blaming them, or even vilifying them.

orphan, and stranger signify voices that make unconditional claims on us (revelation as law, as command) from a standpoint beyond (transcendent to) the horizons of our most natural (not necessarily but possibly evil) concerns both as individuals and as communities. In the context of our reflections here, *we* just might be the church.

Levinas begins his treatise with a set of contrasts (*TF* 21–22):

politics	morality
history	eschatology
war and violence	peace
reason and philosophy	revelation

The left-hand column signifies immanence, the development of human thought and practices within the horizons of the human, the all too human. That reason and philosophy are linked with war and violence may seem strange. But like Kierkegaard before him, Levinas (and most of what is called postmodern thought) knows that when human thought calls itself "Reason," this is all too often little more than self-congratulation and even self-deception. Particular and contingent ideas and interests pass themselves off in this way as expressions of some universal and timeless truth. Like MacIntyre, Levinas has learned to ask, "Whose justice? Which rationality?" (see chap. 10 of *TF*). Since reason in the Western tradition, especially in modern times, has been largely about mastery and possession, Levinas is not surprised to find a link between reason and philosophy, on the one hand, and war and violence, on the other. Put in terms of the Cold War or the current struggle between jihadist Islam and "the West," neither side finds itself short on compelling "reasons" that justify the violence and war they plan for and perpetrate. Often enough, these reasons are theological in nature. In an almost cynical view, this is the story of history and politics as Levinas sees it.

Almost? Yes, because history and politics so conceived are not the whole human story. There is also revelation and the transcendence it expresses. The faces of the victims, the widow, the orphan, and the stranger (refugee, emigré) say "No!" to the nexus of history, politics, war, and reason from a place or nonplace outside that unholy alliance. This is not *cosmological* transcendence, the metaphysical claim that God is distinct from the world (though monotheism presupposes cosmological transcendence).[5] It is *epistemological* transcendence insofar as it affirms a teaching that does not come from human reason in either its individual or its social forms; it is *ethico-religious* transcendence insofar as it affirms a justice, goodness, and divinity and thus imperatives that are irreducible to the values of the self or of society.[6] They intrude uninvited as the authoritative claims that place the self and society in question.

For Levinas the primary mark of revelation is immediacy. "The immediate is the face to face" (*TF* 52). In philosophical usage, *immediate* is not a temporal term, a synonym for "right away." Rather, it signifies knowledge that is, obviously but crucially, unmediated, knowledge that is direct, unfiltered, undistorted through any addition, subtraction, or interpretation by the knower. In many Western traditions, both philosophy and theology have aspired to attain to immediate knowledge by appeal either to intuition or to method, whose task is to filter out all the filters through which the real gets filtered.

Kant famously challenged this possibility by arguing that the human mind itself is a filter. Its forms and categories are the a priori conditions of any possible experience; they compel the world to appear otherwise than it truly is (see chaps. 1 and 7 of *TF*). During the nineteenth and twentieth centuries, Kant's view of the a priori as ahistorical and universal, in other words the view that we all have or rather are the same filter, was replaced again and again both in Europe and in the United States with analyses of human understanding in terms of a variety of historically particular and contingent lenses that mediate the world to us. Gadamer's theory of tradition is but one example of this systematic denial of immediacy.

We could say that Levinas is operating in a philosophical climate whose orthodoxy is the denial of immediate knowledge. So is he a

5. Cosmological transcendence is the claim that God and the world are existentially asymmetrical. That is, there can be God without the world (which is a free creation and not a necessary emanation), but there cannot be the world without God. Pantheism can be defined as the view that the relation is symmetrical: there cannot be the world without God and there cannot be God without the world. The two are related like fire and both the heat and the light that emanate from it.

6. I have discussed these three modes of transcendence in Merold Westphal, *Transcendence and Self-Transcendence: On God and the Soul* (Bloomington: Indiana University Press, 2004). While they are not at all mutually exclusive, I argue that epistemic transcendence is deeper and more fundamental than cosmological transcendence and that ethico-religious transcendence is the deepest and most fundamental of all.

heretic who simply refuses to accept this overwhelming orthodoxy? Yes and no. *No*, because he agrees that what passes as knowledge and understanding in our culture is richly mediated. For just that reason he refuses to grant ultimacy to any of those rationalities that legitimize the self and its society in their natural (not necessarily but possibly evil) self-assertion. Rather, he affirms revelation as the in-breaking of a voice (the face that speaks) from beyond those rationalities. It is immediate not because those who come face-to-face with the other are not well equipped with prejudices (in the Gadamerian version of Kant) in terms of which they can interpret the widow, orphan, and stranger in ways that do not disturb their own sleep;[7] rather, it is immediate because it has the power to break through those preunderstandings, challenging them and calling them into question. It refuses to fit without remainder into the Procrustean bed of our preunderstanding.

Is this a return to the kind of intuition in terms of which the claim is raised, "No interpretation needed"? No, for it is not the claim that our beliefs and understandings are mirror images of the real (the face of the neighbor or the Word of God) unaffected by our prejudices. It is rather the claim that there is a voice that, while remaining true to itself, has the power to break through those prejudices, to disrupt and unsettle them, to call them into question, to show that they need to be revised or replaced, that they are always penultimate and relative, never ultimate or absolute.

Here's an example I like to use. It comes from Sartre's analysis of our relations with others, which is part of the background of Levinas's own analysis. Sartre quotes from the final pages of Faulkner's *Light in August*. A gang of rednecks has just castrated Christmas, a black man. Faulkner writes:

> But the man on the floor had not moved. He just lay there with his eyes open and empty of everything save consciousness, and with something, a shadow, about his mouth. For a long moment he looked up at them with peaceful and unfathomable and unbearable eyes. Then his face, body, all, seemed to collapse, to fall in upon itself and from out the slashed garments about his hips and loins the pent black blood seemed to rush like a released breath. It seemed to rush out of his pale body like the rush of sparks from a rising rocket; upon that black blast the man seemed to rise soaring into their memories

7. Wakefulness is a major metaphor for Levinas.

forever and ever. They are not to lose it, in whatever peaceful valleys, beside whatever placid and reassuring streams of old age, in the mirroring face of whatever children they will contemplate old disasters and newer hopes. *It will be there, musing, quiet, steadfast, not fading and not particularly threatful, but of itself alone serene, of itself alone triumphant.*[8]

In Levinas's language, the face of the dying man speaks loudly. It shouts in the midst of the silence. It is immediate because, although his killers are well armed (pun intended) with interpretive prejudices (in both the Gadamerian and everyday sense of the term) that render their action not only permissible but highly commendable and even heroic, the gaze of the dying man breaks through these "defenses"[9] and makes itself heard in a way that will echo "in their memories forever and ever."

A more overtly theological example is to be found in Barth's distinction between revelation and religion. Religion represents in both theory and practice the human, all too human, response to revelation as the threefold Word of God: Incarnation, Scripture, and preaching.[10] Religion is always revelation mediated by a variety of historical and cultural factors. But revelation is immediate. It is the continual breaking in of the voice of God that calls religion, in Barth's case especially the Christian religion, into question. Revelation is the subpoena of piety to answer before the rigorous cross-examination of a voice we can never assimilate to our own. It continually awakens religion from its dogmatic slumbers. Thus Barth can speak of "The Revelation of God as the Abolition of Religion."[11] Actually, Barth calls revelation the *Aufhebung* of religion. This is not its abolition but the process that renders religion relative and penultimate in spite of its perennial tendency to take itself to be absolute and ultimate.[12]

8. Quoted in Jean-Paul Sartre, *Being and Nothingness: An Essay on Phenomenological Ontology*, trans. Hazel E. Barnes (New York: Philosophical Library, 1956), 406 (p. 526 in the Washington Square Press 1992 paperback ed.); emphasis in Sartre.

9. The killers doubtless think they are somehow acting in self-defense, and in this way they defend themselves against the voice of their own consciences.

10. Karl Barth, *Church Dogmatics*, trans. G. T. Thomson (Edinburgh: T&T Clark, 1936), 1/1§4.

11. Karl Barth, *Church Dogmatics*, trans. G. W. Bromiley and T. F. Torrance (Edinburgh: T&T Clark, 1956), 1/2 §17.

12. In his translation of §17, Garrett Green calls attention to this mistranslation. See Karl Barth, *On Religion: The Revelation of God as the Sublimation of Religion*, trans.

A phrase that Levinas uses to express this immediacy of revelation is καθ' αὐτό (*TF* 51–52, 65, 67, 74–75, 77). It is the Greek term
of which the Latin *per se* is the translation, and it means simply
"through itself." That which expresses itself καθ' αὐτό expresses itself,
it does so in person, and it does so on its own terms. "Manifestation
καθ' αὐτό consists in a being telling itself to us independently of every
position [prejudice] we would have taken in its regard, *expressing
itself*" (*TF* 65; emphasis in the original).

We can think of the couple we met in chapter 9 in the office of a
marriage counselor. The goal, it will be recalled, which was not reached
automatically or even easily, was to let the parties in turn express
themselves καθ' αὐτό, to tell the story from their point of view and
to be heard in just this way, unfiltered, unedited, undistorted. In the
therapeutic context, this goal can (sometimes) be reached, at least for all
practical purposes. In the theological context, it is always an unfinished
task, approximated to a greater or lesser degree as we become better or
worse listeners to the Word of God, but while in revelation God speaks
to us καθ' αὐτό, our hearing is always religion, that is, human, all too
human. Revelation is immediate; religion is mediated. That is why all
Christians can affirm with the Reformed tradition that the church is
ecclesia reformata, semper reformanda secundum verbi dei.

Levinas gives us a more general version of this formula: every
human community—political, religious, or whatever—needs to be
open to the voice of the other in its immediacy, and this task is one
we can never be finished and done with. To listen and to hear—
these are task words, not achievement words. Since the churches
in their hermeneutical finitude and fallenness are human, all too
human, communities, Levinas's account can be helpful in theological
self-understanding. Indeed, the voices that interrupt the sleepy self-
assurance of the churches can indeed be the voices of the least of
these suffering sisters and brothers (Matt. 25:31–46)—the widow,
the orphan, and the stranger (immigrant)—and we can hear the
voice of God in their faces if we are willing.

But it is the voice of Scripture, not that of our culture, that tells
us how important these are in the eyes of God, and it is the voice of

---

Garrett Green (New York: T&T Clark, 2006). But "sublimation," with its psychoanalytic
overtones, doesn't really capture the Hegelian overtones of *Aufhebung*. If one could
use a phrase to translate a word, we might say that *aufheben* means to put something
in its proper, subordinate place. "Relativize" might capture this sense.

Scripture in and through which God performs many other speech acts. Moreover, it is the work of the Holy Spirit to continually break through our complacent prejudices and shortages of wisdom in and through the words of the Bible. It is not enough to affirm the role of the Spirit in the production of Scripture (see Eph. 3:5 and 2 Pet. 1:20–21 above); it is equally necessary to listen for and to hear what the Spirit says (present tense) to the churches. Word and Spirit. As this slogan becomes practice and not just theory, the divinely transcendent voice of Scripture will become incarnate in human language, and we will hear the very voice of God in our finite and fallen interpretations.

How scary! How wonderful!

Index